Praise for *Emergence*

"Barbara Marx Hubbard is the quintessential teacher for the Great Shift that we are living in. Her work inspires, enlightens, and provides a practical framework for moving beyond the limitations of our personal and cultural history to becoming co-creative Universal Humans. This book is a simple, powerful primer for how to do just that. The steps are clearly described and illustrated in Barbara's transparent, personal, and deeply authentic style. If this book were your only guide to spiritual evolution, it would be enough to bring you all the way home. Brava, Barbara!"

—Joan Borysenko, PhD, *NY Times* bestselling author of *Minding the Body, Mending the Mind*, coauthor of *Your Soul's Compass*

"This timely handbook for unlocking our own highest potential by one of the great visionaries of these troubled times offers evidence of the power within all of us to assist in global evolution when we adopt a better way to 'be.' *Emergence*'s central message is provocative and compelling: when you change your life, you change the world."

—Lynne McTaggart, bestselling author of *The Field*, *The Intention Experiment*, and *The Bond*

"*Emergence* sets forth a step-by-step path to shift our identity to our divine essence and to bring forth our unique creativity for the re-creation of our world."

—Gerald Jampolsky, MD, and Diane V. Cirincione, Ph.D., authors of *Change Your Mind, Change Your Life*

"An essential guide to nurturing the inner wisdom that lies within us all."

—Peter Russell, author of *From Science to God*

"A pure note of positive possibility for our common future . . . It offers the kind of spiritual depth needed for the times ahead."

—Paul H. Ray, Ph.D., coauthor of *The Cultural Creatives*

EMERGENCE

Also by Barbara Marx Hubbard

Books

52 Codes for Conscious Self Evolution: A Process of Metamorphosis to Realize Our Full Potential Self (with CD)

Conscious Evolution: Awakening the Power of Our Social Potential

The Revelation: A Message of Hope for the New Millennium

The Hunger of Eve: One Woman's Odyssey toward the Future

The Evolutionary Journey: Your Guide to a Positive Future

The Evolutionary Communion: The Sacred Way of Conscious Evolution (guidebook with CD)

DVDs

Our Story

Visions of a Universal Humanity

What Is Conscious Evolution?

EMERGENCE

The Shift from Ego to Essence

BARBARA MARX HUBBARD

FULLY REVISED AND UPDATED

INTRODUCTION BY NEALE DONALD WALSCH

HAMPTON ROADS

This edition first published in 2001 by Hampton Roads Publishing Company, Inc., with offices at:

665 Third Street, Suite 400
San Francisco, CA 94107
www.redwheelweiser.com

Sign up for our newsletter and special offers by going to *www.redwheelweiser.com/ newsletter/*

ISBN: 978-1-57174-674-0

Library of Congress Cataloging-in-Publication Data available upon request

Cover design by Jim Warner
Text design by Debby Dutton

Printed in the United States of America
MAL
10 9 8 7 6 5 4 3 2 1

The evolutionary impulse is the consciously experienced choice-in-action to take form and become the whole universe. It is the energy and intelligence that burst out of nothing, the driving impetus behind the evolutionary process, from the big bang to the emerging edge of the future. And that impulse is active right now, throughout the life process, and at every level of your own human experience.

—ANDREW COHEN, *Evolutionary Enlightenment: A New Path to Spiritual Awakening*

Evolution is in part a self-transcending process—it always goes beyond what went before. And in that novelty, in that emergence, in that creativity, new entities come into being, new patterns unfold, new holons issue forth. This extraordinary process builds unions out of fragments and wholes out of heaps. The Kosmos, it seems, unfolds in quantum leaps of creative emergence.

—KEN WILBER, *A Brief History of Everything*

Therefore the coming of a spiritual age must be preceded by the appearance of an increasing number of individuals who are no longer satisfied with the normal intellectual, vital, and physical existence of man, but perceive that a greater evolution is the real goal of humanity and attempt to effect it in themselves, to lead others to it, and to make it the recognized goal of the race. In proportion as they succeed and to the degree to which they carry this evolution, the yet unrealized potentiality which they represent will become an actual possibility of the future.

—SRI AUROBINDO, *The Hour of God*

There is emerging from out of the mist of myth, religious and scientific, a new thought, so new, so ancient. This thought is that the transcendent God of History indwells each of us as us. Our relation to all avatars is that of younger siblings, sisters and brothers who are awakening at last to the awesome and exhilarating truth, the final fact of the ultimate covenant. We are the heirs, the operative expressions of divinity Itself, now!

—SIDNEY LANIER, *The Sovereign Person: A Soul's Call to Conscious Evolution*

CONTENTS

Foreword by Neale Donald Walsch ix

Introduction xix

The Guide to the Emergence Process xxix

INFANCY

STEP ONE: **Entering the Inner Sanctuary** 3

STEP TWO: **Contemplating the Glory of the Beloved** 13

STEP THREE: **Incarnating** 25

STEP FOUR: **Inviting the Beloved to Take Dominion** 35

STEP FIVE: **The Bliss of Union of the Human and Divine** 45

CHILDHOOD

STEP SIX: **Shifting Our Identity** 59

STEP SEVEN: **Transferring Authority** 75

STEP EIGHT: **Educating the Local Selves**   85

STEP NINE: **The Repatterning of Life**   103

YOUTH

STEP TEN: **Fulfilling the Promise**   117

Epilogue   137

Afterword   145

Glossary   147

Bibliography   153

Foundation for Conscious Evolution   157

FOREWORD

Well, here it is.

This is the book you've been waiting for.

This is the book that provides an answer to the question, "How do I get from where I am to where I want to be?"

This is the book that finally addresses the question, "And how does the world?"

In startlingly clear and strikingly simple terms, this book lays out a road map to not only a better tomorrow, but also a better Here and Now. That makes it both conceptually stimulating and imminently practical. In other words, it's the kind of book you can get excited about, and it's the kind of book you can use.

Here you will find a wonderful guide to experiencing your highest self. A step-by-step instruction. A flashlight at dusk, a candle in the dark. And you did not come to this book by accident. It is all part of a process of your own emergence, and of the emergence of the entire human race.

To its immense credit, this book does not claim to be the way, but simply to be a way. That's important; otherwise it could turn into dogma—which is the last thing that its author would want.

Now let's talk about that author for just a moment.

I have known Barbara Marx Hubbard for a number of years. I have known of her for a great many more. That is because Barbara's life and work have touched the world in such enriching ways.

A philosopher and futurist of the first rank, she has written; lectured; facilitated workshops and retreats; acted as a quiet consultant to political, business, and spiritual leaders; and placed the wealth of her mind at the disposal of the human race in countless other ways, large and small, adding much to the treasure that is the human experience, and considerably enhancing it.

Anyone who has read one of her books knows what I mean. Anyone who has heard her lecture understands my comments perfectly. Anyone who has been deeply touched and changed forever at one of her workshops nods now in gigantic assent.

And anyone who has asked for her help in thinking through the problems of our times, assessing the challenges and the possibilities of our tomorrows, or charting a course for our future knows why Barbara Marx Hubbard is regarded across the United States and around the world as a breathtaking visionary and a brilliant conceptualizer whose insights astonish and excite the human heart and so are sought after everywhere.

What is presented here is not only a new way to understand our human history but a way to magnificently create the history of our tomorrows, changing forever our very idea of what it means to be human.

Here is a short but fascinating story of our species and the path it has taken, as well as the path it now has an opportunity to take. Here is also an emphatically compelling story of individual transformation—a story of Barbara Marx Hubbard's own work with this material, of her own spiritual experiment—that winds up presenting us all with a path to what could well be our own grandest human experience.

We can become something that we never were—and have always been. We can create something that we could not have imagined—and that we've always dreamed. We can produce something on this planet that we never thought possible—and that we always knew was probable, sooner or later.

We can do this if we will allow ourselves to explore together and to take together the journey to the ultimate realization of our human nature and the total experience of our divine nature, which are one and the same.

This will take a sincere willingness to deeply understand both the prior limits of our human experience and the unlimited wonder of our human potential—and to turn what we have come to understand into the functioning realities of our daily life.

And it will take opportunity.

That's what you're holding in your hand. If I were called upon to describe this book in one word, I would say *opportunity.* Because that's what this book represents. And it is an opportunity that you have called to yourself.

So now, read what you were meant to read. Know what you were meant to know. What you have always known— and are now ready to act upon.

Your own emergence is at hand.

Neale Donald Walsch

Author, *Conversations with God, The Mother of Invention: The Legacy of Barbara Marx Hubbard and the Future of YOU* and most recently *The Storm Before the Calm: Book 1 in the Conversations with Humanity Series*, as well as other numerous best-selling books

ACKNOWLEDGMENTS

Emergence is dedicated to my eldest daughter, Suzanne. Years ago, she asked me a critical question: "What do we know about the developmental path of the Universal Human?" We began to search together to discover the pattern of our own Emergence. How did it happen that each of us had evolved so far beyond the worldview and state of being in which we were born? We probed our own life paths, sharing our earliest memories, our unitive experiences, our woundings, choices, awakenings, and passionate desire to more fully express our unique creativity through joining with each other. Suzanne, a weaver, mother, and gardener, is discovering and recording a "Blueprint," a new lens that serves as a portal for us to discover the actual process of our own personal Emergence through "whole-oriented consciousness." We are deep partners in the Emergence Process.

I also dedicate *Emergence* to my beloved sister Patricia Ellsberg, who is a remarkable social-change activist, strategist and evolutionary coach. We have been best friends our entire lives. As the wife and partner of Daniel Ellsberg, she helped him release the Pentagon Papers to the press, which contributed to the ending of the Vietnam War and the downfall of a US president. She inspired me to realize the full value and significance of *Emergence*, and I am delighted she is joining me in teaching the Emergence Process widely throughout the world.

Emergence is dedicated with everlasting gratitude to Patricia Gaul, known as the "mother" of the Foundation for Conscious Evolution, who has done the major work to serve the foundation's purpose to "Communicate, Educate, and Activate Humanity's Potential for Conscious Evolution." With her husband, Norman Kremer, she has directed and produced the Humanity Ascending documentary series, including *Our Story* and *Visions of a Universal Humanity*.

I also dedicate *Emergence* to my friend Stephen Dinan, CEO of the Shift Network, a global multimedia company that is producing my seminal work, including teleseminars of Emergence and Agents of Conscious Evolution. Stephen is producing "Birth 2012: Co-creating a Planetary Shift," he is a visionary architect of the emerging world. I also thank Devaa Haley Mitchell and the whole Shift Network team for their gracious assistance.

Emergence is also dedicated to Sidney Lanier, founder of American Place Theatre in New York City and author of *The Sovereign Person: A Soul's Call to Conscious Evolution*, whose love of me and faith in the emergence of the "sovereign person" in each of us has drawn me forth and supported me for so many years.

Very special and ongoing thanks to Neale Donald Walsch, who urged me to write this book, who was its first editor and publisher, who has supported me in all my work and countless others through his inspiration. As a popular author and teacher, he is helping millions to change their image of God, humanity, and our cultural story, empowering us to become the greatest version of ourselves that we can be. He has also written *The Mother of Invention: The Legacy of Barbara Marx Hubbard and the Future of YOU*, recounting my life journey, starting in the future.

Special thanks to Sister Judy Cauley of the Sisters of St. Joseph, who has undertaken to systematize and bring into teachable form the whole field of conscious evolution, to offer it to people seeking to form communities and hubs to understand, embody and act as agents of conscious evolution.

Special thanks to Holly Norman, who with my sister Patricia greatly helped me edit this new version of *Emergence*. Holly has been an embodied practitioner of Evolutionary Consciousness, both through her work in corporate America and in her daily life, and has made a significant contribution to the teachings in Emergence.

Special thanks also to Ron and Victoria Friedman of the Vistar Method of circle formation, who are offering us guidance in forming a global network of evolutionary circles to encourage our conscious evolution.

Also deep gratitude to the "Seed Group" of the Santa Barbara Conscious Evolution community, who invited me into the resonant field that launched the repatterning of my life and with whom the first edition of *Emergence* was written. The whole community tested the Emergence Process for the first time, forming resonant core groups to practice the shift from ego to Essence. Special thanks to Bonnie Kelley, Lucky Sweeney, and Jeanie Derousseau, who were leaders in this effort.

I add my special thanks to Teresa Collins and Marshall Lefferts, who as executive directors of the Foundation for Conscious Evolution brought forth the first major teaching through Gateway to Conscious Evolution and trained guides throughout the world.

Also to Carolyn Anderson, who was my campaign manager during my successful political campaign to have my name placed in nomination for the vice presidency on the Democratic ticket in 1984 and who with John Zwerver cofounded Global Family, pioneering with me the core group process. She, John, and Katharine Roske coproduced *The Co-creator's Handbook: An Experiential Guide for Discovering Your Life's Purpose and Building a Co-creative Society* and recently served as editors for *52 Codes for Conscious Evolution: A Process of Metamorphosis to Realize Our Full Potential Self* (a vital next step after *Emergence*).

Also, while becoming a second "mother," birthing myself and others as young Universal Humans, and partnering with my eldest daughter, Suzanne, I am so inspired by all my beloved children, Woodleigh Marx Hubbard, Alexandra Morton, Lloyd Frost Hubbard, the late Wade Hubbard, and all my grandchildren: Danielle Hubbard, Peter Hubbard, Jarrett Morton, Renee Brown, Savannah Rose Hubbard, Clio Nelson, and Liam and Teagan Hubbard. I want to thank my late husband, Earl Hubbard, for his magnificent art and inspiration in our codiscovery of the new story of our birth as a Universal Humanity.

There are countless colleagues and evolutionary leaders who have deeply inspired me, including Jonas Salk; Abraham H. Maslow; Buckminster Fuller; Dr. Thomas Paine, deputy administrator of NASA; Gene Roddenberry, originator of *Star Trek*, and Jean Houston and Hazel Henderson, the first co-creative women I had ever met who influenced my life forever. A recording of my conversations with Houston and Henderson was published in the book *The Power of Yin: Celebrating Female Consciousness*. We are all members of a worldwide community of evolutionary and transformational leaders.

Finally to my first benefactor, the late Laurance S. Rockefeller, who supported this work for ten years, bringing it to a point of fulfillment.

INTRODUCTION

The Emergence Process is an evolutionary path leading to the development of ourselves as more co-creative "Universal Humans." Ten progressive steps, which unfolded in my own life journey, guide us from within to make the fundamental shift of identity from ego to Essence, from our egoic, separated local self to our essential, spiritual self, our true nature. Gradually, the anxious, driven egoic self falls in love with its own Essence and invites its own higher self to take dominion within the "household of selves." We overcome the fundamental human illusion that we are separate from each other, from nature and from Spirit. We cultivate within ourselves the next stage of our development that has in the past been embodied only in extraordinary mystics and saints and is now approaching a "new norm" in millions of people.

The Emergence Process is designed precisely for this moment in human history when we are facing two radical unknowns that we have never encountered before.

One is *devolution:* the destruction of our own life-support system, the collapse of major social systems, the suffering of billions of us, as well as other species, as we overpopulate, pollute, fight, and bring human civilization and other species toward catastrophe. Something is dying. Something is over. Self-centered human behavior and unlimited growth in a finite Earth is not sustainable. We are the generation born in the midst of the end of one phase of human evolution.

The other unknown is *conscious* evolution: If we can learn to evolve ourselves and our social systems, we see a future of immeasurable possibilities through the integration of our spiritual, social, and scientific/technological capacities, leading toward the emergence of a co-evolving, co-creative humanity with powers we used to attribute to gods.

We are the first species on Earth to be aware that we can cause our own extinction or our own evolution by our own actions. This is the greatest wake-up call that humanity has ever had. This is a global crisis/opportunity pressing us toward the "birth," the emergence of something new, something higher than we have ever been before . . . or toward devolution or destruction!

The choice is evolve or die!

It appears that we are at the threshold of the first age of conscious evolution; this is the evolution of evolution itself from unconscious toward conscious choice. For billions of years, nature has been evolving, crisis after crisis, shift after shift, toward greater complexity, consciousness, and freedom. From single cell to multiple cells, from animals to humans. But we humans in the 21st century are the first of all species to be able to place ourselves *in the evolutionary story, as conscious participants in it.* And know that we are causing our own extinction or evolution by our actions.

How do we learn to evolve consciously? The best response is by studying how nature has been evolving for billions of years.

From this context of billions of years of evolutionary transformation, we see recurring patterns. For example, we learn that crises precede transformation. Problems are evolutionary drivers. Nature has been taking jumps through greater synergy, making new whole systems out of separate parts. As systems become more complex, they rise in consciousness and freedom. When a system reaches a chaos point, "it is launched irreversibly on a new trajectory that leads either to breakdown or to breakthrough to a new structure and a new mode of operation," as described by Ervin Laszlo in *The Chaos Point*. From this perspective, we can view the terrible crises that could destroy human civilization and much of Earth life as potentially generating the dangerous, painful, yet necessary birth of ourselves as a more mature, loving cocreative species.

Why would the process of evolution stop here? With us?

It's clearly not stopping. We see many signs of the rise of empathy, spirituality, and creativity. There are social innovations and new solutions arising in every field of endeavor. Perhaps the most fundamental and world-changing capacity of all is the maturation of our "noosphere," the mind sphere, the "thinking layer of Earth." It is bringing all human knowledge together and making it accessible to everyone. It is connecting us with one another beyond all existing governments and power structures. It is fostering empathy throughout the world as we become aware of and feel one another's suffering everywhere through mass media and the Internet. It is through the noosphere that we can blow up worlds or create worlds, make new life forms or destroy all life. The noosphere is our planetary nervous system. It is growing minute by minute, connecting us in a new collective brain, mind, and heart of unprecedented genius, power, and connectivity. Over four and a half billion people have cell phones! Facebook is the third-largest nation in the world. Every day new ways of being in touch with one another are growing. When you see this phenomenon of global connectivity with "evolutionary eyes," you realize that this is a natural maturation of the planetary nervous system. Our biosphere produced human life, which created language, built cultures, systems, and technologies that are now connecting us in the noosphere. It is like an invisible new social organism linking us heart with heart and center with center. Metaphorically speaking, our crisis is the birth, *potentially* the birth of a more evolved human, a Universal Human, one capable of co-creating a new planetary civilization and eventually a Universal Humanity.

What is a Universal Human? It is one connected through the heart to the whole of life, a person awakening from within by a deep heart's desire to express and give his or her gifts into the world. A Universal Human is attracted to the future progressing toward the unknown, imbued with a mysterious sense of what's emerging, seeking to join with others to co-create a new and better world. It is a type of person who has expanding consciousness and awareness that the universe is evolving and so are we.

Those of us drawn to becoming Universal Humans are actually spiritual/social pioneers building a more compassionate and co-creative culture that could welcome the kind of humans we are becoming.

Let's imagine ourselves as a baby just after birth. As newborns we are panicking. We are cut off from our mother's resources. We don't even know how to breathe! We have to do this quickly, or we will die. The panic is real. However, as newborns, as we find ourselves held in our mother's arms, feeling her heartbeat, our nervous system integrates. We relax, begin to coordinate, overcoming the natural fear of separation. We take our first breath, open our eyes, see our mother for the first time . . . and smile. We find that we do have the capacity to breathe, nurse, eliminate, and, of course far more.

The same may be true of humanity. Hope arises when we recognize that we are all members of this one planetary body. When we realize that if we coordinate with one another, we do have the technology, resources, and know-how to make it through together. We feel an innate love for our Mother Earth or God or Essence. We even feel loved by the larger process that is creating us. We are encouraged and realize that we have the capacity and the heart's desire to survive, thrive, and evolve.

The Emergence Process is an evolutionary path for just this type of human, for those of us who are awakening right now to something new within ourselves and are yearning to give our greater gifts to heal and evolve our world.

What is a vital key to our evolution now?

If we could identify one fundamental characteristic in human nature that has been the cause of so much of our suffering, it is this: the illusion that we are separate from each other; from nature; and from Spirit, the divine, or universal creativity.

This illusion can be overcome, because it *is* an illusion. It can fade quickly, especially when cultivated in the Emergence Process in communion and resonance with others.

In *Emergence*, I use a biological analogy to describe the process. The fulfillment of this process is a "Universal Human," a next stage in the evolution of our species. The "adult Universal Human" is a new attractor that we intuit and may be moving toward but have not yet fully manifested. Our full "adulthood" as a Universal Human will happen only in a mature society in which we have developed new systems of cooperation and new capacities of co-creation now barely emerging.

First comes **Conception.** This can happen at any age. It is marked by sudden awakenings, higher spiritual experiences, and inspiration from masters, avatars, great teachers, and inspired beings. These unitive flashes of higher experience lift us out of our daily identity as creature humans eating, sleeping, reproducing, and dying. We may forget these experiences, but if they are not suppressed, they will reoccur naturally, and we find that we cannot ever go back to our old limited self-identity.

Then comes **Gestation**. Once we are awakened by spiritual or mystical experiences, we seek deeper inspiration in our daily lives. We read books, attend classes, learn practices of many faiths, meditate, pray, and search, evolving in consciousness, ever less comfortable with our current mind-set and often lifestyle, relationships, religions. Something new arises within us, pressing us onward.

We are entering the fateful moment we are calling **Birth**. It is the birthing of ourselves toward our Universal Humanhood. We no longer want to seek outside of ourselves for yet another inspiration. We feel that Source coming from within ourselves. The birthing process begins with the choice each person can make to shift from being a seeker of external higher power to the recognition that each of us is an expression of that higher power within.

Then comes **Infancy**. We are just barely able to realize who we are becoming. We are attracted to our Essential Self that first awoke during our Conception and Gestation, training ourselves to focus on that deeper Essence of our being. We dwell in a protected Inner Sanctuary, cultivating "the bliss of union" of the human and the divine, or deeper reality, experiencing the grace and joy of its presence within us. We are initiating a process of incarnation toward full embodiment as a whole being, a Universal Human.

Then comes **Childhood.** At this stage we make the fundamental shift or phase change from ego to Essence. We recognize what mystics have always taught: We are expressions of universal Designing Intelligence. The Essential Self is the guide that has been guiding us. We are an expression of the inner voice we have been hearing. We are an incarnation of the Beloved we have been seeking. We begin to function on a limited scale and in a protected environment as our own Essential Self integrating and educating our egoic, local selves.

Youth comes naturally as we grow out of our childhood as young Universal Humans. It occurs when we find our life purpose, what we are born to do, and we create small communities or circles of partners and pioneering souls, beginning our larger work in the world. It is like a second puberty. We are shifting from maximum procreation to co-creation, from self-reproduction to self-evolution. We experience vocational arousal! Sexuality expands into "suprasexuality," exciting us not to join our genes to have babies, but to join our *genius* to give birth to our full potential selves and our greater work in the world. We stabilize our awareness of our essential nature as an expression of Spirit, the higher power, or whatever name we call it. In this stage we "come into form" in the external world, in the co-creation of projects of all kinds. We work in all fields to re-create a world that is sustainable, compassionate, and expressive of our greater creativity and love.

Youth prepares us for the **Adult** stage as Universal Humans. This emerging stage, imminent in us now, can only fully appear as we, the pioneering crossover generation, successfully pass through this period of transition and build a sustainable, evolving planetary civilization.

Emergence comes from my own personal experience as a very young, still growing Universal Human becoming newer every day at eighty-two!

THE GUIDE TO THE EMERGENCE PROCESS

What follows is a journey. It unfolds in ten progressive steps to take you through your Infancy, Childhood, and Youth, on your way to becoming a Universal Human. You may use it to take your own journey and to find out about mine. I describe here my journey which I am still exploring, offering vital guideposts from the spiritual experiences of my life. I have left a trail of clues so that others might make it through this thicket a little more easily, step by step. As you read through the Emergence Process, you are invited to take this journey with me. It may lead you to places that you have never gone before.

Following are suggestions on how to use this guide to the Emergence Process:

- First, read through each of the ten steps to understand the entire Emergence Process.

- Set aside a sufficient period of time each day to create and be in an Inner Sanctuary as you experience each of the ten steps of the Emergence Process. This can be a place you simply imagine. If you wish, you can also create a physical space of beauty and peace in which to mediate and journal.

- Allow yourself to consider making a profound commitment to your own Emergence Process. If you feel ready, set your intention to realize your full potential in this lifetime. Many of us discover that the Emergence Process is a lifelong evolutionary journey that deepens every time you revisit it.

- Create a special journal to record your journey and any insights and inspirations for your continuing evolution. It is best to do this when you are in a state of contemplation in your Inner Sanctuary.

- If you are so moved, invite one or more kindred souls into an Emergence Circle to do the process with you, sharing each step along the way.

I congratulate you and cheer you on as you begin this very powerful process and join me in Emergence!

Love,
Barbara

INFANCY

Entering the Inner Sanctuary

Infancy! This is the time when the newly born Universal Human emerges from the womb of self-centered consciousness. We begin to realize our new identity as our own higher, Essential Self. We break out of the limits of our egoic identity and, in innocence and humility, make room for something new.

The Story . . .

On my sixty-ninth birthday, I made the choice that started me on this journey, which is now transforming my life. The scene was Marin County, California; it was a cold, rainy January and February 1999. I stayed warm next to my fireplace while a steady rain came down, giving me a feeling of inwardness and protection. I was alone with a huge project—to write a conscious evolution curriculum for Universal Humans, an educational framework that begins with the Void and covers the origin of the universe through to the present and beyond.

My dining room table was stacked with neatly piled books on every phase change in the story of evolution, written by authors whose work had inspired me for many years. The room was filled with the "noosphere," the thinking layer of Earth, our global brain/mind/heart, the evolutionary impulse of humanity.

Yet, in spite of this rich and supportive environment, I found myself to be driven and compulsive about my work, trapped in a struggle to get the job done. Although I was urging and encouraging others to experience a positive future in their lives, now I was not at peace and could find no place of rest within. I realized I had to stop my life to make way for something new.

To begin, I decided to arise before dawn and devote three hours every morning to being silent and alone, long enough to allow something new to happen. In my early morning silence, I created an Inner Sanctuary, a safe inner space where I felt protected, secure, empty, uninterrupted by my own demands or anyone else's. This was a place as profound as the quietest monastery or cave, a place I created within and around myself. I let there be soft music, candlelight, flowers, and above all, peace and quiet.

I set aside time "out of time" to be in the Inner Sanctuary. But even at the thought of doing this, my compulsive, egoic local self was prickling. I was bombarded by its loud complaint: "We don't have time; we'll never get the curriculum done." My driven local self always felt "behind" no matter what time I woke up and began my work.

But I persisted. Every morning, I simply sat in silence, open and empty, listening to the crackling fire and the rain drumming softly on my roof. I offered my burdens and responsibilities as sacrifices at the threshold of the Inner Sanctuary, literally laying them at the entrance before I entered into my meditation. I imagined myself as a pilgrim in front of a temple, purifying myself before entering. When the compulsive local self prodded me with "You forgot to call so-and-so!" or "What are you going to have for lunch?" I resisted, no matter how magnetic the pull. I felt like the mythological Odysseus, strapped to the mast of his ship to prevent himself from succumbing to the temptation of the Sirens. My egoic, compulsive need to be working was my temptation. I let it go by.

Within the Inner Sanctuary, I created a special place for my journal writing and a quiet time following my meditation to gain more intimate access to the wise and Beloved inner voice, the Essential Self, that had guided me all my life. This was a voice I'd heard many times, sometimes coming to me in intuitive flashes, but more often, when I wrote in my journal, it flowed as a stream of ideas emerging from a deeper awareness than my conscious mind. Whenever I felt this flow of inspiration, I relaxed, listened, felt joy, and received guidance from my Higher Self. It was a motivating presence that had been with me since my origins as a young girl living with my family in New York City. I had been raised with no religion, no metaphysics, no idea of any kind of greater existence, and so this inner voice became the agent of transformation in my life.

While I had no idea of this then, I know now that all of us have this inner voice. It is the Higher Self, the Essential Self, within each of us—which *is* each of us—and it is communicating with us all the time. Sometimes we hear it, and sometimes we don't, but it is never really silent.

My childhood having passed, and my experience with this Beloved inner voice having deepened through the years, I wanted to expand my experience of this inner voice. To start this Emergence Process, I created my own Inner Sanctuary, both internally and as a physical space. I went to my writing table and allowed the inner voice to write. One morning, shortly after I began this practice, these words flowed from my pen:

> There are no demands on you now but to rest in my arms—the Inner Beloved—who is one with God. Rest in me. Release all cares. Your work is over as a separated local self. . . . I am now preparing the way for you to enter into the world as who you really are. Rest in peace. Do your yoga and your journal as you rise at dawn each day for the next twenty-one days. Be still. This is your time of communion. Do not hesitate now. By remaining still for long enough with me during these twenty-one days, the alchemical process will be set at the next stage of your evolution as a Universal Human.
>
> I want you to rest in the arms of others who are also transcending now. You are not alone. Feel their strength

and know that you are part of them, they are part of you, and that your function is to be an expression of them. You are part of all who are transcending. Patterned within all of you is a new humanity. This is the purpose of the curriculum you are writing.

Follow precisely the path I dictate to you for the next twenty-one days. That is what it takes. Everything has been prepared for you to take this step alone. Then you may join other co-creators as an expression of the new human. But you must take this time now to secure the incorruptible connection.

Now is the greatest leap of faith for you. Have utter faith in me. Achieve deep peace. Be prepared for a great force to enter your life to do this work. It cannot enter till you have achieved deep peace. Your reward for peace that can only be achieved by faith is contact with the force and the forces waiting in the wings.

I was thrilled with this guidance. An electric excitement awakened a deep sense of expectancy in me.

The Guidance . . .

Your own Essential Self, as you access it through your meditation and writing in the Inner Sanctuary, will offer you guidance, inspirations, and practices as well. That guidance, when added to the guidance in these pages, will create for you a unique manual for the Emergence of the Universal Human you are now becoming.

I strongly advocate cultivating an inner receptivity, an inner listening and attunement to the signals of the Essential Self. These intuitions are the way the deeper self informs us and guides us.

Create an Inner Sanctuary

To begin, set aside time to sit quietly every morning in peaceful contemplation for as long as you can with your journal beside you. This may be familiar if you have meditated before; any practice you are used to will work to quiet the mind and prepare the inner field. The Emergence Process is not a substitute for any basic practices you are already doing but rather an extension or deepening of them.

Set aside a period of time for an at-home spiritual "advance." You can do this simply by arising earlier than usual every morning and using the extra time for this practice. Peter Russell, author of *The Global Brain Awakens, Waking Up in Time,* and *From Science to God,* calls his morning hours his "daily Sabbath," a time for God to come through the whole way. Choose a time in your life to begin this "advance" when you will not be distracted or interrupted by any major life crisis or transition, such as a journey, a divorce, a move. Once the Emergence Process is deliberately started, it is preferable not to stop it abruptly. If the early morning hours don't work for you, choose another time. The Dalai Lama meditates at least four hours a day and travels all over the world. We don't have to be in a cloister to begin this process, but some kind of intensification of focus is essential. Remember, you are preparing for a rendezvous with destiny!

Focus Attention on the Essential Self

In your silent time, recall as much as you can of the guidance or inspiration you've already been in touch with—the actual feeling tone of your intuitive experience—and also any qualities you remember about this evolutionary impulse that has motivated your process of transformation. You may recall those earlier experiences. Remember how warm and safe you felt. Feel the intimacy and compare it to the feeling of anxiety and compulsiveness that can characterize a local self.

If you ask your Essential Self to come into your consciousness, it will signal you in some way or another, not necessarily as mine does, and not necessarily in written words. It may happen in flashes, insights, images, or hunches. Watch for synchronicity to show up in your life, a phenomenon described by Carl Jung in his book *Synchronicity: An Acausal Connecting Principle* (1969) as "the meaningful coincidence of two or more events, where something other than the probability of chance is involved." Intuit the meaning of synchronicities. This is critical. Notice everything with a heightened awareness. The signals will come, because it is the very heart's desire of the Essential Self to communicate with you. When you ask it to communicate more clearly, it will—one way or the other. Expect the unexpected, and anticipate the new!

Release the Pressure of Time Running Out

There is nothing you need to do or accomplish in the Inner Sanctuary. See if you can feel "off duty." Every time you feel the pressure of the thought of time running out, release it. Don't fear; you will still be able to be on time. But releasing the pressure provides the vital freedom needed in the Inner Sanctuary for the Essential Self to come forth. It is vital that you inform the anxious aspects of your local self that there is "all the time in the world," or even better, that you reside in eternity. This is what Ram Dass meant when he said, "Be here now."

In the past, I always had good reasons for not taking the time to practice in this way. Looking back, what I was really telling myself was "I don't have time to be born!" I know now that it's an affliction of local self-consciousness to get its priorities backward, and that there is nothing more important we can do than give highest priority to our own process of Emergence. There is no greater gift we can give to those we love than ourselves evolved.

Sometimes when I am walking or sitting silently in nature and I want to feel "off duty," I turn on my internal answering machine to pick up the stream of incoming messages from the local self—that endless "to-do list" that seems to pop up whenever I attempt to be still within myself. I place on the internal answering machine an outgoing message to assure the local self that its requests have been recorded and it can relax, knowing its "urgent" messages will be responded to at a later time. I have trained my memory to go back, after my walk or meditation, and check those incoming messages. In this way I don't forget what the local self had requested and can respond as I choose.

Journal

Throughout the Emergence Process, keep a journal of messages from your Essential Self so you can recognize and establish a relationship with your Inner Guide. This was a key practice in preparing me for my own Emergence. I have tracked this guidance since I began keeping a journal at age eighteen and have continued to record inner messages all my life, accumulating more than 175 volumes of personal writings as of this moment in time.

Gradually, as my Emergence continued, I realized that there was no reason to refrain from accessing that voice all the time, in my knowing, speaking, and acting, as well as my writing. I found that when I don't access the voice, it wells up and signals me through a sense of depression or confusion. Depression is often a signal of a growth impulse that is attempting to attract your attention. The key is to seek the deeper meaning behind the pain and respond.

To begin with, as in all the steps that follow, create and place yourself in your Inner Sanctuary. For your first journal exercise, write and describe from memory any key experiences or insights inspired by your Essential Self. This will help you get acquainted with your Essential Self by bringing it to your conscious attention.

What did the voice or inspired thoughts tell you? What did it feel like? Describe any messages or insights that you have received, any qualities you have noted that characterize the Inner Guide.

Once you have done this, try this exercise: Write a letter addressed to "Dearly Beloved," or whatever name you choose for your Essential Self. Describe your current situation as precisely as you can, the good and the apparently difficult. Ask the most important questions you may have, as clearly as you can; then release all thought, have no preconceptions. Develop the habit of a poised mind, like a sailboat on a calm sea waiting for the wind.

Our purpose here is precise. It is to establish direct contact with the inner voice, the still, small voice of God expressing as your Essential Self. Start writing any sentence as the inner voice, and see what unfolds. Do not edit, judge, or correct anything. If nothing comes, that is fine. Continue to be still.

If you have been hearing an inner voice and writing in your journal before, this process will be relatively easy. If you have not yet tried this, simply follow the steps with no expectations. Find your own way to connect to your Inner Guide. It may be through other paths than words, like a felt-sense or deep intuition. This much I know for sure: Whatever happens will be helpful. Everyone has within a deeper, wiser, all-knowing self.

Contemplating the Glory of the Beloved

With the creation of an Inner Sanctuary, we have established the field of readiness for our Emergence as Universal Humans. In the stillness, we may have felt the presence of our Essential Self or perhaps a sense of expanded awareness and wholeness. At this stage, we are like the biological infant when it begins to sense itself as a separate entity, a "self." In our Infancy as Universal Humans, the self we are becoming aware of is the Essential Self, the Higher Self. Now, in this next step, we are ready to fully contemplate this Essential Self in its more personal form, the Inner Beloved, and bring our focus to the specific qualities and wisdom of this all-knowing inner presence.

The Story . . .

Although I have heard and been directed by this inner voice of my Higher Self for most of my life, I had never focused my local self's attention directly on it until undertaking this process. Before, I asked, listened, heard, wrote, and then acted according to what I'd heard. I communed with God and Christ, but all the while feeling the divine, the deity, to be outside and beyond myself—separate.

The inner words I heard passed through me to the page on which I wrote but did not become me. I had never contemplated the actual presence of my Higher Self, so that I could feel it, consume it, incorporate it into my flesh and bones—incarnate it—until now.

As I turned inward toward this presence, I began to experience a sense of homecoming, of peace and safety, yet at the same time, I was filled with excitement and anticipation. I noticed the qualities of this Beloved Self who had been signaling me from afar for so long.

She—for the presence, to me, was distinctly feminine— was not merely an abstracted, "floating" inner voice. Nor was this voice identifiable as the impersonal God of the cosmos, or even as a Christ presence. Whereas before, I had experienced this presence as Christ or God, now, as I placed my attention on a personal feminine presence day by day, "she" seemed to become more real, almost tangible to me. She seemed to be myself! Yet my sense was of a magnificent presence, far beyond my current personality or gender. What I now experienced was a full range of attractive and familiar qualities of the Beloved that had been flickering at the edges of my consciousness all these years.

At first, the presence I felt was a huge shimmering field of light, but as I contemplated deeply, more personal qualities entered my awareness. She is a visionary, a seer. Yet she is warm, motherly, cozy, tender, like the mother I lost when I was twelve. She loves me unconditionally. She knows everything I ever ask her.

The Essential Self, the Beloved Presence that I am, the source of the early unitive flashes I had, was becoming familiar. I realized that I know this Essential Self better than I know my anxious local self. I am in love with this self, in contrast to my irritated, pressured, and compulsive ego. Yet this self, whom I now recognized as omnipresent in my consciousness, was not revealed until I, from the viewpoint of my local self, put attention on it in the Inner Sanctuary.

The experience in the Inner Sanctuary began to pervade my day with its current of joy. As I went about my work, I felt as though an alchemical process had begun to turn on within me. Warm currents of electricity, very pleasant and calming, flooded my physical experience. Ripples of joy swept gently through me. I noticed that a light euphoria had replaced my chronic anxiety.

My nervous system stopped being irritated by compulsive thoughts. The constant feeling of being rushed, slowly but surely, faded. If I awoke with the old twang of anxiety, I recalled my experience of the Beloved, and the nervousness seemed to disappear.

To my delight, I noticed that this process in itself was self-rewarding. Like the proverbial carrot on the end of a stick, the peace and pleasure I was now experiencing in my daily life motivated me to spend more time in the Inner Sanctuary to contemplate, feel, and enjoy the glory of the Beloved.

Several days into the process, I wrote in my journal, beginning in the voice of my local self and addressing the Beloved as I had always done:

Dearly Beloved,
I have come home to you now. I have created the Inner
Sanctuary in my little apartment and am here now with
my communion and meditation—the fire, the music,
the flowers, the flickering candlelight, the symbol on the
dollar bill I have placed in a frame (the pyramid with
the cosmic eye and the phrase novus ordo seclorum—
"new order of the ages"). You have infused me with your
joy at last. I felt this morning, when I awoke, that in-
stant nervous anxiety, but the connection with you was
there, strong enough to withstand the fluctuations of the
nervous system. I felt my nervousness batter against the
connection like waves against a mighty wall. The wall
stood. The protection was there. The door was closed. I
feel deep in my solar plexus that something is healing, is
knitting together.

I had been feeling a deep sense of anxiety that I could not bring my mission to fulfillment; my fear was that "I" would fail. Of course, I realize that this fearful, anxious "I" was an aspect of my local self, yet my local self is the one who has been carrying the burden of searching and executing. It was my local self who received signals and guidance and tried to act on them. Now the local self was being absorbed into the Essential Self and began to relax and release its anxiety.

I ask now, Beloved, what is your word for me today?

The answer came:

Every morning, as you write in this intimate way, you will be tapping into the glory that is being revealed in you. Do not think at all about your morning. We have a surprise for you that will bring joy into your heart and light into your eyes.

What is this surprise?

The surprise is you now writing directly as a Universal Human to the Universal Human in others. It is your coming out of the closet as yourself in such a way that others will be encouraged to do the same. Above all: Don't think about this.

It is thinking that is your "problem." Each morning after your communion with me, I want you to write without thinking until the Universal Human that you are is writing directly to the Universal Human in millions of women and men. Give it no thought. Let it unfold. Write as long as the pen will flow. You are uncorking a Big Bottle here! This is what we promised you. This is the reward of union with Me. It is union with yourself. It is the life and the light and the love that you are speaking directly, now.

This kind of writing is the next step after so-called channeling. It is a direct and personal expression of the Great Creating Process itself. It is the process of the incarnation of deity. It is God expressing as you.

You are not to leave the Inner Sanctuary—ever. You are to carry it with you wherever you are. In this Sanctuary you emerge fully as a Universal Human.

It is important that you come to feel connected to your Essential Self at all times. The disconnect comes when you lose the feeling connection with who you really are.

Can you feel Me now?

Yes, I can. I feel a sort of gentle excitement and anticipation.

Yes, that excitement is Me, the One who is you, who loves you, who guides you. It is this One who is writing. She is now coming through the veil. Feel the veil dissolve. Feel Me dissolve the barrier between you and Me until we become as One. Let Me come forth into your consciousness until I am in dominion over your whole body-mind. Let Me through, Barbara. Let yourself dissolve into Me. Let your self-centered mind be completely absorbed into Me. Let Me heal and regenerate your macular degeneration [age-related loss of vision] so that you can see clearly again. I told you that you were losing your sight because you had narrowed your vision to become useful in the world. This was useful, but it is no longer necessary. What is needed now is your full-blown, full-frontal presence as Me emerging as who you truly are.

The Guidance . . .

The next step in the Emergence Process is very simple, yet profound. Often, as I have mentioned, we have recognized the divine outside ourselves. We have prayed to the higher power, we have worshipped God in many forms, or we have identified ourselves with the infinite, nondual reality, losing all sense of a personal self.

Occasionally, mystics experienced the divine within, but very few of us could hold this state of consciousness. Instead, we relied on priests, master teachers, or divine beings who seemed far beyond our personal, intimate knowing. Now, due to the phase change on planet Earth, when humans are gaining Godlike powers to co-destroy and co-create, our relationship with the divine is changing. We are no longer children; we must become conscious participants in the process of creation. And, in fact, countless people are becoming ever more connected to the larger whole, both internally through spiritual attunement and electronically through information media.

I believe that as Universal Humans we will gradually learn to incarnate the divine, realizing that each one of us actually is an expression of the process of creation. We are *that* in unique form. We are not, and never have been, separate from the Source of our being. As we cross over from ego to Essence, we recognize that we always have been one with the Great Creating Process itself, or God.

The Emergence Process is based on the experience that the Essential Self in each of us is "ripe and ready" to come in the whole way—if we make the conscious choice to focus our intention upon that deep self within. Now is the time of our Emergence. So, during the time you have set aside for being in the Inner Sanctuary, consciously turn the sunlight of your attention inward to focus upon that deeper self in whatever way you experience it: the God-within, the Beloved, the inner voice or guide, the intuitive wisdom that has been—one way or the other—guiding you all along. We are calling it the Essential Self. Use any name that is familiar to you.

Turn the attention of your local self away from its worldly considerations toward this inner presence that is connected to non-dual Reality. This takes focus and high intention. Every time the local self tries to escape into separation—into some distracting thought of what needs to be done—turn it back to the Essential Self. You will find that you know and love this self and, in fact, are magnetized by this self. It is your Essential Self! But it has been awaiting the attention of the local self's conscious regard. You will recognize it because it is profoundly familiar, even if you have never been fully aware of it before.

Essential Self–Contemplation

The key practice, once the Essential Self emerges in consciousness, is Essential Self–contemplation. To do this, spend as much time as possible allowing the magnetic needle of your attention to drift inward and upward to focus on the felt presence of your inner self. Contemplate the specific qualities of Essence that you most love. Affirm that these qualities are you.

By this attention, you will materialize the very highest qualities that you seek in yourself. These are all the qualities that the ego has been seeking by its efforts in the world. Joy. Peace. Security. Love. Wholeness. Wisdom. All these qualities are continuously present. The more you focus on them, the more they penetrate your being. Your attention manifests them in your awareness and incarnates them as you.

Do this, not only in the Inner Sanctuary but also during the day. Expand your consciousness to include awareness of your Essential Self in everything you do. When you are walking down the street, notice the presence, feel the warmth, attune to the inner voice. Gradually, we learn to keep the practice alive all day, always.

Become the Director of Your Attention

See if you can train your attention to seek a new resting point, a new base state. Instead of letting it flicker and then alight on current problems or situations, gently guide it inward and upward toward the Beloved presence within. You'll know that you have succeeded when a feeling of warmth and pleasure infuses your nervous system.

Staying with this practice creates a new "strange attractor," a magnetic field within you, as you learn to be sensitive to this excellent biofeedback signal. The moment you feel the pang of ego expressing through anxiety, irritation, or anger, stop. Breathe. Return to Essence. We are training the inner muscle of attention to be spontaneously attracted to

Essence as a new norm. For spiritual athletes, this is a vital and ongoing practice.

Forget Your Local Self

Don't be forced by the local self to pay attention to some pain, problem, or circumstance. We know that whatever gets our attention gets us, and so it follows that whatever quality of being we focus on grows within us. As the local self is occupied contemplating the glory of the Beloved—the radiant presence of the Essential Self—it stops focusing on its problems. It loses its grip on your psyche and begins to become self-forgetful. This is very good news!

The longer you can keep your attention on the Beloved, the more steady and ongoing will be the alchemical process that this focus brings. The emotions of warmth and joy are signals that the process is continuing.

We now know that emotions have an underlying biochemical process, fully coordinated by the body/mind on a physiological level. We have also learned that grief or anger or any prolonged negative emotion can cause downtime for the immune system, directly affecting the health of the body.

The Design Is Perfect-Making

Whatever happens may not be what we would have consciously chosen. Often it is not. But when we examine it in the Inner Sanctuary, we find that at the deeper level the situation is not perfect, but it "perfects" us to face it, if we choose to accept the challenge. We may experience trauma, tragedy, obstacles, but they can be interpreted as opportunities for growth, designed for our own perfect-making.

The Inner Beloved can be called upon to offer the wisest possible response to the crisis, whatever it is. At this stage, everything is meaningful. Apparently difficult experiences can be reinterpreted as precise openings for self-evolution. Facing the conditions of life both exercises and strengthens the Beloved, calling forth the deeper joy of our Essence underneath the struggle and pain.

Since I have committed to realizing my full potential in this lifetime, I choose to interpret everything that happens to me as an opportunity for self-evolution. I tell myself that if I did not need to learn from a particular experience, I would not be given it. With this understanding, I prefer to face a painful experience now rather than later, because if I face it fully now, I will learn the lesson and not have to deal with it at some future point.

Discipline of Relaxation

The sign of local self-dominance is tension. The local self feeds on stress. Whenever you notice that familiar twang of the nervous system, it is a biochemical signal that the local self has taken over, and that you are separated in consciousness from your Essence. This is the fundamental cause of the chronic anxiety that afflicts most of us in the modern, secular world.

The minute you feel the tension, stop, breathe, smile, and refocus on the Beloved. You are gaining two skills. The first is becoming director of your attention. The second is consciously fostering the alchemical process that is now beginning to work toward your transformation. You are in charge of your attention, which is vital to your Emergence.

Journal

Once again, enter your Inner Sanctuary. Contemplate your Essential Self in its more personal form, the Beloved.

Try writing about a challenge you are facing and how you can interpret it as an opportunity for growth. In what ways does it call forth your strength and lead to your own evolution? What guidance or wisdom do you receive from the Beloved? Describe the evolutionary impulse that has motivated you to transform.

In your journal, continue to describe any experiences you have had of your Essential Self. Contemplate the specific qualities of Essence you most love. Affirm that these qualities are you. What is your experience as you contemplate the Beloved? What does it feel like?

Write without thinking. Let the words flow. Use whatever language works best for you. We do not want to be divided by semantics. There are no fully agreed-upon words to describe these experiences. I tend to use evolutionary words to bridge the gap between the spiritual and the scientific worlds. Each of us can make a contribution to the languaging of our experiences so as not to divide but to include.

STEP THREE

Incarnating

As infants we are maturing. Just as a newborn baby begins to live in the awareness that it is no longer in the womb but born into a new sense of self, we emerging Universal Humans leave behind our former self-consciousness and become aware of our Essential Self much of the time. An infant experiences comfort and peace when held in the arms of its mother. Its panic is calmed as it learns to breathe, nurse, eliminate, and coordinate its newborn self. It begins to smile and feel at home in the "new world" beyond the womb.

So, as we mature as infant Universal Humans, we gain a sense of assurance in our new identity beyond the womb of self-consciousness. The Essential Self begins to come in the whole way. We gain a feeling of peace and joy as the local selves relax their fears and let go of their efforts to control.

The Story . . .

As I spent time in the Inner Sanctuary, contemplating the exquisite qualities of the Essential Self, and as I either allowed problems to pass through or considered them as gifts and sought their meaning, the Beloved began to come in further, to substantiate within myself, to incarnate.

In this process, I could physically feel this deeper self as a vibrational field penetrating through my heart and down into my solar plexus, where the knot of anxiety of local self's concerns seemed to dwell like a cold and resistant tumor of trouble, regardless of external situations. The Beloved "warmed the cockles of my heart," as they say, and even began to melt the cold, hard knot of clenched emotions in the solar plexus.

I noticed that, as the Essential Self came in further through the attention of the local self, various aspects of the local self relaxed their grip on the conscious mind. In fact, much to my delight, I found that my compulsive local self was lifted up into the vibrational field of the Beloved.

In the process of incarnating, we discover that the sense of separation, which the ego so often feels, is actually not real.

As I have said, the fundamental human problem out of which other problems spring is, I believe, the illusion that we are separate from each other, from nature, and from Spirit. As we continue to place our attention on the Essential Self, the illusion fades. We remember our deeper identity most of the time. This identity, of course, is not a personal ego but a personal Essence, a unique expression of unconditional reality, or God.

In the Inner Sanctuary, it felt as if a disturbing pattern of my local self—the compulsive thoughts—was being erased quickly by the vibrational field of the Beloved. The local self couldn't quite remember what it wanted, for in fact, it didn't really want anything anymore! Why would it, when it was beginning to enjoy unconditional love, which is the inner ambiance of the Beloved?

The experience was like coming into the warmth after having been out in the cold. There by myself, on the rainy mornings in my little condo, I was experiencing a natural "high." Only instead of taking a substance to induce a high, I was becoming the new substance myself! This natural, sustainable high, I realized, was becoming available as a new norm.

I felt as though I was falling in love with my Essential Self, an inner love affair. A deep and genuine experience of happiness, independent of my work, infused me, and this startled me. The "starter button" of compulsive thoughts—Do this! Do that!—commanding me at six in the morning and before I went to bed at night, stopped stressing my nervous system. The workaholic aspect of my local self subsided. For the first time in a long time, I felt at peace.

I had not been this happy since I was a child, before my mother's death when I was twelve. Over the years, I had scarcely realized this, placing my attention on my life's purpose rather than upon the evolution of my self. True, my vocational purpose was my pleasure, but, as I said, my work had been taken over by attachment and compulsion. Now, at last, there was a shift of focus from doing to being, a shift that eventually frees vocation from the egoic attachment, allowing it to come forth unimpeded by anxiety and self-criticism, as a flow of creativity.

As the inner process took hold, the outer work began to take shape effortlessly. Plans that I had been working on for years began to manifest easily as I spent time in the Inner Sanctuary. The work on the conscious evolution curriculum flowed. I was literally organizing every major concept I had ever had, complete with books, references, and quotes from key thinkers illuminating the evolutionary story from the Void through the Big Bang and into the present and beyond. Professors and academics became interested. People were excited and awaited each module.

I was no longer feeling cut off but in fact was becoming connected at a deeper level than I'd ever experienced before. (This experience foreshadowed the complete repatterning of my life that occurred later in the process, demonstrating how inner integration leads to outer manifestation of our deepest values and aspirations.)

I continued the journal writing and began to describe the situation in my morning letter to "Dearly Beloved."

The purpose of this writing is to bring Essential Self through. I am not to write anything for others until I can sense, touch, feel, and be that steady Presence. I am to become substantial as myself. This is known as bringing yourself "through the veil."

I now understand what is happening to me. There was in me such an overriding compulsion to "fulfill my mission" that I continually put the purpose of being my

Essential Self second, not first. Now, by grace, I have finally taken the time and space to both bring my Essential Self through the veil and to write the conscious evolution curriculum.

Even as I wrote, I felt a flash of the old anxiety pulling at me. There was a little tug at the center of my solar plexus that seemed to say, "Get to work . . . it's 8:30 a.m.!" The Inner Guide responded:

When the pull of anxiety comes, let it be. Be still. Put this purpose first. Do not act upon the temptation to "get things done" at the expense of nourishing, flourishing, nurturing the Presence that I am. When you feel the anxiety, just let it be.

This is the initiation. On the subtle planes, it is the process of transubstantiating yourself through communion with the divine.

I had never "Put This Purpose First." The desire to fulfill my mission, given me by the inner voice, compelled me to action, in such a way that I did not fully remain connected to the Source of the guidance. That has been the crux of the disconnection, which must be healed for this initiation to complete itself.

I wrote:

I humbly surrender the temptation to manifest in the world for the reality of being the manifestation I am

seeking and unfolding the expression from that vantage
point. This is my calling now.

I was seeing how my personal experience related to the bigger picture of conscious evolution and to the quantum shift many of us are undergoing. Since our world is evolving, so obviously are we.

Experienced more widely and to their fullest, the Emergence Process, and other similar processes in various forms, may well engender an actual alchemical transformation on a planetary scale. When we learn to stay in this state over time, we will live in a continuous, sustainable resonant field of co-creation, creating a new culture for a new humanity—a Universal Humanity—that reflects our higher state of being.

The Guidance . . .

In the Inner Sanctuary, we continue to place our attention on our Essential Self, which we experience as a vibrational energy field, the radiant Presence of the Beloved within. This presence enters our inner awareness, releasing stress and anxiety, filling us with a gentle joy, lightheartedness, confidence, and a growing trust in the process beyond the confines of our rational minds. When an addictive thought pattern arises in the Inner Sanctuary, such as "I am a failure," it is quickly erased in the vibrational field of the Beloved already established.

Now we enter a new phase in our development. When the local self, by its own intention, repeatedly places its attention on the Essence of its being, we begin to vibrate at a higher frequency. The Essential Self seems to change our very physical substance from density to lightness, from contraction to free-flowing energy. We experience our Essence as substantial. It feels as though the Essential Self is incarnating, entering our body/mind and transforming it as our local self resonates to the higher frequencies of the Essential Self. We are entering the next stage of the continuing incarnation of the divine in human form.

A. H. Almaas, the revered spiritual teacher and founder of the Diamond Approach, in his seminal work *Essence* (1986), tells us that Essence is "not only a concept, an image, an archetype, or a state of mind. Rather, it has precise and definite physical characteristics." Essential Self incarnation is, in other words, really transubstantiation—a change in the substance of our being.

Put This Purpose First

The key practice at this stage is to continue putting the purpose of being Essence first, not second. This does not mean we stop doing everything else in our life. It simply means that whatever we are doing, we keep our primary focus of attention on the Beloved within. In the Inner Sanctuary, continue Essential Self contemplation and practice radiating the warmth and presence of the Beloved within yourself. Do this especially if a local self acts up and you feel anxiety, or lack of self-esteem, or rejection. Radiate the presence directly upon the wounded self, like a mother embracing a frightened child, comforting and calming.

All day, every day, as you leave your meditation, make of your life a continuous process of placing your attention on the presence of the Essential Self. The local selves will begin to experience a deep attraction, a desire to remain in the presence of this beneficent being, rather than to stray outward in anxious efforts. The magnet of your attention begins to draw to it wayward thoughts. They will continue to occur, but you will find that as long as you keep your attention on the source of your inspiration, the local selves will release their grip on you. You will begin to feel a new freedom from anxiety, pressure, and compulsions.

Close the Door

As was described in the previous step, local selves have a way of escaping out the back door of the Inner Sanctuary. Just as I am contemplating Essence, a disturbed local self will send in a thought—"We must get busy writing the curriculum!"— that begins to pull my attention away from my focus on Essence. That prickly feeling of irritation clouds the Inner Sanctuary. Before I know it, I am interrupting my time in the Inner Sanctuary, dialing a phone call to some professor!

For me, it became necessary to declare, without equivocation, that there was absolutely nothing local self could do, on its own, that would bring peace or real satisfaction. No matter what the temptation—one more book, event, or success—it will not lead to fulfillment of myself or the work, if done for the purpose of trying to fill up the emptiness inside. Whenever a local self attempts to get out the door to satisfy itself through manipulation of the external world, it finds it irrevocably closed. No escape! This sounds overly absolute, perhaps, but I found it worked.

Journal

Once you enter your Inner Sanctuary, take time to feel your Essence. Love it. Allow it to substantiate further and further. It will become more real as you place your attention and focus on it.

Describe what you experience as your Essential Self begins to incarnate. What does it feel like when it comes in the whole way? What is your lived experience of this higher frequency?

What can support you in placing your attention more continuously on the presence of your Essential Self? What are the beneficial effects of putting this purpose first?

Continue to communicate with your Essential Self. Often I simply asked, "Dearly Beloved, what do you have to say to me today?" I stop thinking and hold a poised mind. I begin without having any idea or thought as to what to write. Even as the first word comes into my mind, I do not know what is coming next.

This is good. The attitude of surprise is helpful and fun. The writing flows like an inner script that unfolds when attention is placed on it. The words hold the code of our own evolution. Often they express wisdom far beyond the rational mind.

We learn to anticipate the flow of guidance from the Essential Self, recognizing that this wisdom is our own. Essence is like a wonderful spring of living waters. It fills up daily and wants to be expressed. If it is not expressed, it will signal us by depression, disease, or addictions. The word wants to come forth. The inner voice wants to be heard. Now is the hour of our Emergence!

STEP FOUR

Inviting the Beloved to Take Dominion

As we contemplate the glory of the Essential Self in the Inner Sanctuary and allow it to incarnate more fully within us, the local self, weary of its compulsive behavior, becomes ever more magnetized toward the Beloved. It feels pleasure in the presence of this beneficent, loving energy that draws it forward like a baby to its mother's breast. At this stage the local, egoic personality self becomes so enchanted with the experience of its Essential Self that it freely, voluntarily, even joyfully, chooses to surrender its dominance. It invites the Beloved Essential Self to enter in the whole way, to take dominion within its "household of local selves," the many subpersonalities or aspects of the local self.

There is a time in the life of a newborn infant when it starts to be more comfortable with its physical body. It opens its eyes and learns to coordinate itself—nursing, eliminating, smiling. So, too, as newly emerging Universal Humans, we begin to feel more at home within ourselves, making a conscious choice to come in the whole way as who we really are.

The Story . . .

On a personal level, I began to feel the excitement and fulfillment of a passionate, inner love affair. There was the joy of homecoming, of being "mother" to myself, losing the orphaned feeling I have had since Mother's death. I realized I'd never had a motherly influence in my life from that time forward. I had been a mother of five, and wife, editor, and helper to my husband, and I had passionately loved my work and the work of so many others, but I had never regained a motherly influence in my own life. Now I was about to become mother to myself.

Finally, with the invitation from my local self to the Beloved to take dominion, "mother" came home and held the wounded child in her embrace.

In the journal, the words came:

You have put this purpose first. You built the Inner Sanctuary and placed your attention on me. Through that attention you, local self, substantiated me. You called me in. This process requires that I, the Beloved, be invited by the local self. This is the meaning of free will. This is the meaning of personal conscious evolution. This is the substance of the transformation open to every human being on Earth. I am now, by grace of your choice, to give you the reward.

The reward is union with me, the ever-present, ever-loving, and all-knowing divine self of every human being on Earth. Rest your attention in me so that

*I can infuse you minute by minute with the elixir of
the substance that actually does transubstantiate and
transfigure you.*

I knew a phase change in my process was occurring. First
I had consciously created the space for something new to
happen. Now I was experiencing that something new as the
incarnation of the Beloved, the Essential Self, the God-self.
There came a point when I realized that I, local self, wanted
to fully dissolve my own identity. I no longer could stand being separate. My local self made a momentous decision.

In the Inner Sanctuary, one morning, I deliberately created a new ritual—the Invitation to Take Dominion. I prepared the inner space and began my meditation as usual.
Then solemnly, as though preparing for a marriage, I, as my
local self, lifting my attention to the Beloved, asked the presence of the divine to take dominion within me.

I freely gave up all domination as a local self. I realized
that the illusion of separation was just that—an illusion.
At that moment of invitation, like a bride preparing for the
bridegroom, I declared my heart's desire for union with the
Beloved. From this point on there was no turning back to
the separated self, no returning to my past life of striving.
The invitation to the Essential Self to take dominion is the
greatest single choice I ever made since I had said *yes* to
my vocation. I asked that the union be consummated in me
eternally.

The Guidance . . .

When we make the choice to invite our Essential Self to take dominion within, we are, each of us, crossing the great divide from unconscious to conscious self-evolution. By this choice, we are transforming the nature of evolution, person by person, for evolution proceeds ever more by choice rather than by chance from this time forward.

This is the true meaning of conscious evolution at the personal level. Conscious evolution does not mean that we control evolution by human will alone. It means we humbly seek to be response-able, able to respond, to the deeper patterns of creation for ever-higher consciousness and greater freedom through more complex and synergistic order. It means we work with this awesome tendency in evolution, so often communicated through our inner voices urging us to transcend the limits of our personality and egoic needs.

With this choice to surrender to the dominion of the Essential Self, we set ourselves definitively on the gentle path to the next stage of our evolution. This is the way of love. This is the natural birth process of Universal Humans as we cross the threshold from our self-centered, self-conscious state of being into the next phase of our development.

In the Emergence Process, the local selves do not need to be forced to change; they desire it and long for their own ascension to a higher frequency because it feels so good. The pleasure principle is at work, attracting us to self-evolve, just as it attracts us to reproduce.

On this path there is no need to punish or deny the ego-ic, local self, whether within ourselves, personally, or in the larger world. There is forgiveness of the "sins" of the past. Sin is understood here to mean the illusion of separation from each other, from nature, and from Spirit.

As the illusion begins to fade within us, we can see that the root cause of our cruelty to one another and to other species comes from that illusion. When we actually feel the internal reconnection with the divine, not as an external de-ity but as an internal presence in resonance with the non-dual reality, or the Godhead, equally available within all, we naturally and spontaneously experience the "other" as an Es-sential Self, connected to the One Supreme Reality.

At the level of Essence, we are all aspects of the One, whereas as individual egoic personalities, we feel, and in-deed often are, in a real struggle with one another.

From the vantage point of our evolving selves, we "for-give" our own behavior and that of others as we do of an upset child. Through the process of the incarnation of the Essential Self, the separation is gradually healed, and the childlike human matures to become a conscious participant in creation, that is, a young Universal Human.

I do not mean to imply that this is a quick and simple task, only that it is my experience that as it begins to hap-pen to us, we naturally and spontaneously begin to love one another as part of ourselves. But until this kind of self-evolution spreads, there are still not enough people who feel this way, and therefore society, as it is now constructed, is based on separation and competition.

It is up to those who are evolving to create the social conditions, systems, and institutions that support the planetary shift. This is our task.

Our local selves are often very much like lost and wounded children who yearn to go home. This is the basis of my hope. The natural heart's desire of the separated self is reunion with the divine. We are like individual cells in the body of a planetary system undergoing its crisis of birth as a whole. And the crisis of our "birth"—the new conditions that limit one form of growth in the womb of Earth—is the trigger that will hasten the inner maturation of enough of us to shift the tide of history.

In other words, I see our own Emergence as a natural aspect of the planetary shift from one phase of evolution to the next. The path is to start by loving our own local selves and healing the separation between ego and Essence within ourselves. This is the feminine path to the future. It is guided by the feminine within us all, both women and men, for the love of all the children of Earth, its species, and nature herself.

This is time for the Divine Mother to rise up within us and to take her rightful place as co-equal co-creator with the Divine Masculine, which has so brilliantly given us the power to create and destroy, but who can no longer guide that power for us alone.

Let the noosphere, the thinking layer of Earth, sound a clarion call to its feminine voices of co-creation! Let the feminine co-creator, who understands these new powers, join with the masculine co-creator, to lovingly and ethically guide our new capacities to heal and evolve our world!

Releasing the Illusion of Separation

Prepare for the Beloved to take dominion by taking a moral inventory to deliberately release whatever you no longer choose to have happening in your life. (In my case, it was my compulsive, workaholic fear of failure.) Record your answers. Realize that when the Beloved takes dominion, those experiences will no longer be dominant; our contracted local selves are lifted up and transformed.

At this stage we come to the realization that the local self, like an alcoholic, can no longer handle our life, yet there is a higher power that can, and we are ready to turn our lives over to that higher power, our Essential Self, connected incorruptibly to Source. In preparation for the Invitation, we take a moral inventory and prepare each aspect of our personality to release their illusion of separation. Record in your journal whatever you have received that you are now offering up to be dissolved.

Preparation for the Invitation

Now, in your meditation, prepare the Inner Sanctuary for a special event. Place your attention in the household of local selves, the ones who have been asking, seeking, and attempting to follow guidance. Raise your consciousness upward toward the Essential Self, readying yourself to invite the Beloved to take dominion within the household of all the selves—the anxious, the fearful, the driven.

Feel the Beloved radiating its presence upon the primal source of all fear—the great fall, fault, or chasm within, which is the illusion of separation of the human from the divine. Declare that you want to cast the light of truth upon the shadow, the unconscious source of fear within yourself. Normally, in our interactions with others, we radiate our best thoughts and intentions outward and receive energy back from others' responses to what we have given. In support of the Emergence Process, however, we can practice a different kind of interaction, which is consciously radiating the internal presence, the Beloved, inwardly rather than outwardly.

The Invitation to Take Dominion

Remember the attraction for the Beloved and keep returning to the contemplation of the glory of the divine Essence. Now you are ready for the actual Invitation to Take Dominion. This step is a sacred invitation. It deserves special time and attention. Prepare your Inner Sanctuary with flowers, candles, music, if you so choose. Or simply allow the silence to deepen. Give yourself whatever time you need. This is your inner wedding day. As your local self, focus your attention on your passionate desire for union with your own Essence, your feelings of love, of bliss, of joy at being safe and protected. Solemnly, make your vow to release the illusion of separation of your local self from your Essential Self. With all the power of the local self's yearning for the bliss of union, for the fulfillment of *its* desire for love, invite your Essential Self to come in the whole way, to incarnate. Slowly, deliberately, ask for a complete Union of the Human and the Divine within yourself. With dignity and presence, invite your Essential Self to take dominion. Allow the process to unfold. Experience every moment with heightened intensity. When you feel the reality of Essential Self entering into your being the whole way, rest in silence. Let it be. If possible, give yourself extra time after the ritual. Take long walks in nature. Be poised and expectant with a "beginner's mind," no thoughts, no agenda, just innocence, openness, and love.

Journal

Take a moral inventory in preparation for offering your Essential Self the sacred Invitation to Take Dominion. Ask yourself what you no longer choose to have happen in your life. What are you now offering up to be dissolved? Record your answers.

What inspires your local selves to want to surrender their control and release their illusion of separation?

> Declare your heart's desire for union with the Beloved.

> Offer in sacred ceremony the Invitation to Take Dominion.

> Describe how the ceremony unfolds. What is the experience like as your Essential Self takes dominion within the "household of local selves"?

Be aware as you write that you are recording your own inner scripture. Take your time. Nourish yourself. Allow inspiration to flow through you.

Highlight any inspired insights so you can reread them as you would beloved scripture or poetry.

The Bliss of Union of the Human and the Divine

The Beloved has been invited home and is now taking dominion within the household of local selves. In this next stage, for the first time, the Beloved takes the initiative and invites the local selves to come up unto it. With their ready acceptance, the local selves are lifted up unto the Beloved. They enter a Rose Chamber of the heart, and there, in the field of love, they experience the great reward—the Bliss of Union of the Human and the Divine. We are freed in that instant from our illusion of separation from our Essential Self. Just as the newborn rests blissfully in its mother's arms after the trauma of birth, so we experience the bliss of union with our essential, divine self. The higher frequencies of the Essential Self infuse the whole body/mind, accelerating the alchemy of our transubstantiation and incarnation.

The Story . . .

As my own Emergence Process continued, the inner love affair deepened. I arose with excitement every morning and hastened into the protected space of the Inner Sanctuary.

There, almost daily, I experienced a tremendous opening, an infusion of love coming in waves that flood both my heart and my solar plexus region. What had been a somewhat flashing type of joy in the past was now more sustainable and intense. It felt like a sun was shining inside me.

To hold this new experience, I formed a deeper chamber within the Inner Sanctuary and called it the "Rose Chamber of Union of the Human and the Divine." In this new space, I experienced a glowing, rose-colored light. As I remained in the Chamber, this light gently permeated the density of my body, infusing every part. It felt as though the frequency of my body was shifting vibrationally and being transmuted into light.

The unconditional love of the Beloved embraced me so deeply that there was no fear, no anxiety, no death. Nothing but light and bliss and joy. This experience, so often described by mystics, was happening now through union with my Essential Self. In that instant in the Rose Chamber, I released my identity as the local self. "I" disappeared into the light, absorbed by it and remaining in it for some time. When the experience was complete, I felt that I would never leave the Rose Chamber, because the frequencies had imprinted themselves on me.

When I emerged from the experience and entered into what had been my local self persona, that familiar persona was no longer there. My local self had been transmuted by a higher frequency, which had released it from its delusional separation. It felt as though the local self disappeared and then reappeared again but was now transformed by the frequency of that rose-colored light, the Essence of the Beloved.

When the local selves reappeared, they were vibrating with a new frequency gained through the Bliss of Union. I felt lighter. Their density was gone. I could see their positive qualities. The anxious one was gently giving me energy to fulfill my work, urging me onward. The local self that feared failure was asking me to be excellent, while the one that was judgmental became discerning. All of them seemed like facets of the Beloved, rather than their fragmented, negative former selves.

In the bliss of union, the local self gives up the kind of desire that leads to attachment because its desire is already met through the union with the Beloved. Then comes forth another kind of desire—a life-enhancing, happiness-generating desire. It is the desire to self-express and self-actualize through creative expression.

This form of desire guides us as a compass of joy through the density of daily life in the material world. The desire to bring Essence into form is vital to our full Emergence as Universal Humans. It is the process whereby we transform ourselves and the world.

I found that my compulsive desire to "get the job done" was becoming a creative flow of Essential Self expression. I entered a state wherein desire no longer felt personal but was rather the expression of universal creativity flowing through me in this particular form.

Shortly after this experience, these words came forth into my journal:

I am always with you. I will never leave you. Whenever you are in pain, when you feel the nameless anxiety, compulsiveness, and fear that you will not complete the task, stop, breathe, and I will calm your agitated self. I will do more. Since I am now taking dominion within your being, I will take the initiative. I will radiate my presence. I will breathe you up unto me so that your heaviness becomes my lightness; your fear is comforted through our union. This now, I, Essential Self, commit to you. I am no longer the distant presence to be called upon in your journal. I am the passionate lover of you, my local self.

My heart melted with joy.

As I spent more and more time in the Rose Chamber, I could feel the Beloved residing there unconditionally, regardless of what I was doing in my daily life. Whenever my local self reappeared to drive a car or write a book, make a telephone call or give a speech, the frequencies I experienced in the Rose Chamber were with me.

When I interacted with others, I noticed I had a very different effect than I was used to. This new local self, united and infused with the Beloved, could transmit bliss. People recognized the bliss and would often ask me what was different.

This surprised me, because I wasn't intentionally doing anything different. But when I replied, "I've been experiencing the Bliss of Union in the Rose Chamber," they would say "That's where I want to be!" I would then respond, using the same language the Beloved had used with me, "Come up unto the Beloved within yourself."

People were very quickly lifted up, because the field had been established in me, and the readiness was there in them. It's contagious! I found that I could be to other people's local selves what I, as the Beloved, was learning to be to my own. The Beloved does for others what it does for its own local self. The Beloved doesn't care whose selves they are—all are uplifted!

When I shared my experiences of Emergence with friends, I found that many of them were having similar experiences. I realized that I was not alone, that in this process of mapping my own Emergence, I was discovering a developmental path that has generic elements.

We echo back to each other our Essential Selves. We fall in love with one another at the Essence level. This experience vastly accelerates our own integration and Emergence.

The Guidance . . .

As we undergo this next step in the Emergence Process, we are awakened to the memory of an earlier Bliss of Union that we all share. For this is not a new experience, but rather one we are retrieving, a very ancient knowing. Many of us have touched upon this memory in intuitive flashes of oneness, moments of ecstatic reunion with the whole of which we are vital parts, confirming that we all arise out of one universal process of creation. Mystics and saints have inspired us with descriptions of the ecstasy of union with the divine, and most of our religions were founded upon this experience in all its diversity.

We were conceived in the bliss of union of two seeds of life joined in the embrace of our parents and have experienced the ecstasy of sexuality ourselves.

Far from being self-indulgent or selfish, the experience of ecstasy is the incentive and condition that leads us to our full integration as Universal Humans and so is vital to the survival and fulfillment of humanity. Here, the Emergence Process deepens, for as we know, life can be an ordeal as challenges arise and difficulties appear.

What gives us the incentive to overcome obstacles is often the yearning for the bliss of union held out before us. It is our heart's desire, our soul's motivation. It is not abstract; we feel it whole-bodily. The local self finds that its heart's desire is met in this union of the human and divine. Bliss is its reward; it needs no other.

Create a Chamber of Union of the Human and the Divine

When you feel ready, following your own inner guidance, set aside a special day as you did for the Invitation to Take

Dominion in which you create the Rose Chamber and invite the local selves to enter. You can invent your own rituals, images, ceremonies, and meditations for this event. I am sharing the ones that I love, hoping that you will add wonderful new ones, and then share them with me, and with each other. Here is the ritual I have used:

Prepare the Inner Sanctuary once again. You may choose special flowers, music, candles, or incense. Sit quietly and focus your attention on the Beloved. Allow the divine presence to come into your heart and create there a Rose Chamber filled with rose-colored light (or whatever color most attracts you). This heart light is blissful, the radiant presence of the divine within you.

Feel the Beloved residing at the center of the Rose Chamber, infusing the Chamber with its presence. Experience the Essential Self as a radiant presence, glowing and emanating light. Your local selves are now ascending in vibration, merging and becoming one with the Beloved.

In its presence, the local selves are repatterning, attuning to the higher frequency of the Essential Self. Their knots of concern are dissolving, their density is lightening, and their weary selves are being renewed.

The voice of the Beloved is speaking within, now no longer hovering and signaling from afar but alive within your body/mind. Let the local selves merge with the light. Feel the Bliss of Union of the Human and the Divine.

Dwell in the Rose Chamber as long as you can. Return to the Chamber throughout the day. The continual experience of the bliss of union stabilizes the fusion process of the local self and Essential Self.

In the Rose Chamber, the vibrational field of the Beloved penetrates deep within the cellular level, like an internal healer whose hands are vibrating with the frequencies needed to restore and regenerate life. Notice that the alchemical process is accelerating. Currents of joy lift the vibrational field within you.

The longer we stay in the Rose Chamber, the more wonderful becomes the rest of the day. A glow from the Rose Chamber lingers on, infusing daily life with an all-pervading joy. The local selves purr like kittens. They want more of it! Instead of trying to get us to do something outside ourselves, they are now calling us to return to the Rose Chamber! Their deepest heart's desire is gratified.

It has always been for union, whether it is with the mother, with the lover, with God. Now, "God" is found permanently residing as the Essential Self of each newly born Universal Human. "Heaven," or joy, is our natural state at this next level of evolution.

The longer we stay in the Rose Chamber of Union, the more sustainable becomes the native state of happiness. This is not a mind-blowing ecstasy but rather a gentle infusion of peace, warmth, and contentment. In the Rose Chamber, we participate in the world-changing truth of all mystics: The Kingdom of Heaven is within you. It is heavenly in the Rose Chamber.

Follow the Compass of Joy

As you become more adept at the process, this spiritual joy can be summoned by fixing the experience into our nervous system such that it can be replayed at will with a flick of attention. Simply remember the bliss, and the needle of your attention swings immediately toward it. Instead of focusing on a problem or pain, as best you can, concentrate on bliss and joy.

Make a clear internal decision when you feel a disturbed local self arise. Attract its attention to the Beloved. Firmly, decisively, shift your focus to the Rose Chamber. The local self will relax, as warmth infuses the body/mind. We are learning to orchestrate our own inner reality as young Universal Humans.

Presence the Radiance of the Beloved

Moment by moment, during this blessed period of time, keep your attention on the Beloved, and infuse your body/ mind with its presence. It is an inner healer filled with warm, relaxing, harmonizing light bathing the weary, wounded, separated selves. Just as self-consciousness must have been difficult to remember for early humans in the animal world, so cosmic, universal consciousness is hard for us to remember in the midst of the self-centered world. We flicker in and out like flames in the wind.

Be Rigorous

Every time you feel the old patterns of anxiety, fear, or nervousness, stop. Breathe. Focus on the Beloved, and allow that presence to lift you up. We need to slow down to accomplish our rendezvous with destiny. Our inner state of being is largely our choice. We are at cause of our own experience, not at effect of circumstances in the world. This is basic metaphysical teaching practiced here for the specific purpose of incarnating as Universal Humans.

Cultivate Resonance

As much as possible, stay within yourself or with the one or more friends who can resonate with and mirror back to you your Essential Self. Resonance means resounding, echoing back and affirming the highest in one another. It occurs when our hearts are open and we share deeply from our Essential Selves in an environment of safety and nonjudgment.

Do not hesitate to put out the call to others. Share your experience. See whose heart it touches. Others are waiting for you, as you are waiting for them. Each time you share your experience, it deepens in you. The word becomes flesh when spoken. At this stage, we vitally need kindred others to stimulate and recognize ourselves. Have the courage to share your story and experience. Thus you become a guide to awaken the guide within others.

Form an Emergence Circle

If you feel so moved, invite friends to share the Emergence Process with you. Set aside sacred time. Create sacred space, with flowers, candles, incense, music. Sit in a circle. To begin, be silent. Do a meditation or attunement, evoking the Essential Self in each person. Then do a brief "check-in," describing how each of you is feeling right now. Share with one another exactly where you are in your own Emergence, offering gentle encouragement to one another.

It is not, however, a therapy session. The circle is a space to experience spiritual intimacy, nonjudgment, unconditional love, and resonance. Develop your own rituals. When you are finished, close with a blessing. This process acts as a nurturing "birthing field" for young Universal Humans.

Journal

Place yourself in the Rose Chamber of Union. Describe what it is like to be in this "Kingdom of Heaven Within." What does it feel like to dwell there?

Lift up your local selves into this chamber of the heart. Sense their relaxation.

What is your experience of the bliss of union with your divine Essential Self? Feel the ecstasy. What is the felt sense in your body and emotions? Describe this inner love affair.

Allow the Beloved to write to the local selves any poems of love, songs of praise, expressions of compassion. Bask in the ecstasy of union as long as you can every day.

Record your experiences and internal messages. Write from the bliss.

CHILDHOOD

STEP SIX
Shifting Our Identity

At a point in its development, the infant becomes a child. If the first period of life has gone well, and the infant has fully experienced its union with its mother, it can now internalize that love and reach out into the world with confidence. So, as we feel the bliss of union in our infancy as Universal Humans, the maturation process accelerates. A new identity emerges, born out of the fusion of the Beloved and the local self. The young Universal Human emerges.

We enter our Childhood, not as the Essential Self alone, but as the Essential Self expressing through its local self. We are becoming a self-governing, sovereign person in the world, albeit still a limited and protected world. In Childhood we come together as our integrated selves, learning as co-creators to socialize, follow the authority of the inner teacher, educate our local selves, and play at co-creating with one another.

The Story . . .

I continued to spend time in the Inner Sanctuary, experiencing the bliss of union as dominion of the Beloved took hold. I was already familiar with the Beloved; she has been my

companion all my life. Behind the curtain of my consciousness, she had been sending signals. Now, the curtains were
parting to reveal this familiar presence as my Essential Self,
visible and recognized at last. I was flooded with gratitude
and joy.

The inner being that I so loved, that had lifted me beyond
my ordinary consciousness and brought me to the point of
Emergence, is *me*. I had to get used to this identity.

I am aware of the specific moment in time when the
phase change from Infancy to Childhood occurred for me.
It was an instant of profound self-recognition of what had
always been so, but only now was I able to realize it. It required a conscious effort on my part to shift the "I" of identity—where I reside in my internal state of being—from the
one who was asking to the one who knows.

In the Inner Sanctuary, I had already been practicing re-
membering the presence of the Beloved, but now I placed
the "I" of identity in that Beloved presence. This I did as
a conscious act of will and attention. As I made the inner
shift of identity, I could feel the vibrations within me change.
Warmth and joy flooded my being. I found I could exert
choice as to my "inner weather." I could dispel the clouds
and bring in the sunlight with a flick of attention upon the
Beloved as myself.

To anchor the shift, I spoke out loud and then wrote
down a set of declarative statements, including "I am the
Guide who's been guiding. I am the voice I've been hearing. I
am the Beloved that I have loved. I am the Universal Human

I've been preparing to birth. As that, I am here, present now, in every cell of my being."

I recorded these words in my journal and spoke them out loud as part of my practice. Then I felt the words become flesh as they incarnated and filled me with their radiance. I consumed the words. They were alive in me.

As this process continued, I realized that, as the Beloved, I had been hovering, suspended in space, because I didn't want to come into the flesh the whole way. I was afraid of losing my vision, of being trapped in materiality. I had signaled to my local selves to do more than they could possibly do. I remained aloof and put all the responsibility on them for carrying out my signals, which they could only intuit. I sent my motivational signals and guidance, then I disappeared.

Now, the reverse was happening. As I placed my "I" of identity in the Beloved and raised my local selves up unto me, my local selves disappeared and reappeared as aspects of the Essential Self. After my identity had gone through the phase shift, I was willing to take responsibility as the Beloved for full incarnation in all aspects of my being.

The affirmations I had created as positive declarations, both written and spoken, were now taking hold. I experienced an expanded sense of inner knowing. "I," Essential Self, know everything "we," the family of local selves, need to know. I had already found that when I asked, a wise response always came. Now I realize that I am the wise one who had been responding!

A tremendous sense of inner self-confidence arose as I realized that this informed and informing self is always omnipresent and omniscient as far as my own requirements are concerned. There is nothing that I have ever asked the Beloved for which she did not have a wise response. Now that I have recognized myself as the Beloved, I realize that I have the wisdom and can assist others in the world.

This inner wisdom is always transmitting, and I am potentially always that transmitter. I am not an isolated I, but an I that is integrated upward with Source, outward connected with the Essence of others, and onward with the evolutionary impulse of creation toward higher consciousness and greater freedom. But it requires a poised mind, deep centering, and precise focus to stabilize the new comprehensive identity.

My practice over the years of recording the inner voice and following its commands now took a new turn. What began to express was a new, integrated "I"—the Universal Human.

In my journal I began to address my local selves as I practiced holding my "I" of identity as my Essential Self. My practice is to consciously shift from listening and being guided by the inner voice to speaking as that voice. In this way, I learn to act with my ego in service to my Essential Self.

As I write, the very shift of attention sends a vibration of joy through my nervous system. I feel stabilized, grounded through my hand and my pen and the ink as the words flow spontaneously onto paper. I am now writing the words into my flesh and blood rather than simply onto the paper to be later followed by a separated and dutiful local self. I maintain my identity as guide through writing to the local self, the guided. The journal writing changed and became an intuitive affirmation of what is potential. By intending it, we "tend" to manifest it.

Dear Local Self,

I am now the Universal Human who is already here, full, complete, gently instructing the local self. Local Self! I want you to fully know that the being writing this is me, the me you were told to become. I am not writing this as a Christ voice. I am writing this as Barbara, a young Universal Human who is in the same domain as those higher voices you thought were writing through you before. I am, by my full intention and attention, that self in this form writing this now.

Local self, I ask you to release, let go, dissolve, fulfill yourself in me as me. The way I can best assist you is by clearly writing to you as "Me" with my relationship with higher being secured—I am in touch with higher domains of reality from which I draw and, through that, with the Designing Intelligence, and through the Ground of Being, Void, Field of All Possibilities, Pure Awareness, the Godhead.

"I" am the Universal Human. "You" are the still-maturing local self, asking, seeking, fearing, excited, and sad.

I am present now in this writing. I am the one writing. The way we move toward our reward—our integration as a unified being—is for me to hold the field consciously while you, local self, ask me questions. My goal with you, local self, is your full acceptance and fulfillment of your mission through your ecstatic union with me and our unified communion and communication in the world as that.

You are to spend longer times protected from the old thought patterns of the local self until you can stabilize more permanently. The alchemical process is arrested, stopped, whenever an extraneous thought gets your attention. When the thought captures your attention, you collapse and feel the sinking of the Beloved field. It is the collapse of the wave—the nonlocal field you are in— to the particle, the one specific thought that holds you at the moment. Yet you are a co-creator; you are to be supremely active once again in the world. This is your initiation.

The key now is to use profound affirmations continually all day: I am the Universal Human at one with all that is.

At this point in my process, I continued to write in my journal as the Beloved, recording my affirmations and declarations, and returning as often as possible to the Inner Sanctuary to visit the Rose Chamber and experience the bliss of union. But even though I had experienced a profound shift of identity in my Emergence Process, I still found it easy to forget who I am as Essence. The retraining of my nervous system must overcome more than fifty thousand years of programming in the early phase of self-conscious *Homo sapiens,* so I am patient and humble.

When I forget who I am, or feel discouraged, it helps me to recall the whole story of creation. I remind myself that this is not a neutral universe but one with a direction toward higher consciousness and greater freedom through more synergistic order—a 13.7-billion-year trend. I "surf the evolutionary spiral" in my imagination. I feel its irresistible tendency to overcome every obstacle to more life. I am tapping into the "grace," which is that added energy beyond human will that comes from the process of creation itself, from God.

The same force that brought us from subatomic particles to the present is the grace at work to evolve us now. The grace I feel is that overwhelming tide of creativity forever forming the universe in all its dimensions.

The Guidance . . .

A profound phase shift ushers in this first step in our Childhood as Universal Humans. In Infancy, our local self surrendered to the Essential Self and invited it to take dominion, but we had not yet emerged as the new integrated identity. Now we have crossed over from identifying with the local self and formed a new identity with our Essential Self fully integrated with our local self.

The shift of identity from ego to Essence at this stage of development marks the recognition of who we really are, the moment of self-revelation. The veil of separation between ego and Essence is rent asunder. We are the Essential Self, the Beloved we have worshipped—and experienced—from afar. We are fusing the transforming ego and incarnating Essence as an integrated, whole Universal Human. Almaas describes this shift beautifully in *Essence:*

> The shift of identity from personality to essence is nothing but the realization of the true self, the high self of essence. Practical action becomes the action of true being. There is efficiency, economy, simplicity, directness. One fully lives in the world but is constantly connected to the Beyond, the Supreme Reality.
>
> This integration of all aspects of essence into a new and personal synthesis is the pearl beyond price. When the pearl is first born, it is usually not complete; it is the essential child. It is born as a personal kernel. Then it integrates all of the aspects of essence into its very substance. . . . There is balance, completeness, harmony, fullness, contentment.
>
> All inner compulsion will be gone, for the person is realized, and the realization is based on fullness, richness, and value as a mature being. . . . The station of the pearl beyond price is so significant because it is not a matter of a state of consciousness or being; it is rather the condition of the actualization of one's realization in one's life.

Life becomes a process of creative discovery. . . .
The ego does not need to work any more. The creative
process happens on its own.

When we go through the shift of identity, our relationship to God changes from child to joint heir, from passive re-
cipient to active participant, from creature to co-creator. We
become able to respond to the deeper patterns of creation
through the integration of the human and divine within ourselves.

That inner union provides receptivity to the larger design, and our desire to create provides the motivation. We
recognize ourselves and others as newly born Universal Humans. This is, I believe, the next stage of human evolution.
This is the human being that has been heralded and foreshadowed for eons by the great teachers that came before us
to pave the way.

With the shift of identity, we move from witness consciousness to causal consciousness. As the witness, we place
our "I" of identity in the perspective of observer: "I" am not
my body; "I" am not my mind; "I" am not my emotions. I am
simply witnessing the ever-changing phenomenal world.

Once we have shifted our identity from ego to Essence,
we are no longer a witness of the phenomenal world but a
co-creator of the phenomenal world. In this new perspective,
we actually experience that our larger "mind" or consciousness is causing our own experience of reality. The feeling of
personal freedom shifts from a sense of individual, separated

will to one of surrender into a larger design that feels as if it is our own.

In my vision of our potential future, creation is triumphant in its magnificent struggle to evolve from cosmic dust to cosmic consciousness. In a deep sense, this could be a homecoming for God and humans together.

Our evolution has been an awesome journey of almost fourteen billion years. Every entity that ever moved or swam or crawled or flew, every being that lived to reproduce itself, all the vast numbers of species now extinct and presently living, who invented the amazing capability that we have inherited as our eyes, our ears, our organs, our very atoms, molecules, and cells—all those preceding us are represented in our Emergence now. We bow down in awe and gratitude for the past. Without all that came before us, none of us would be awakening now!

The process of shifting our identity certainly requires no less from us than the training an athlete must go through for the Olympics. It requires total commitment, daily practice, coaching from others, self-observation, intentionality, and grace.

Shift Your "I" of Identity to the Beloved

When you check within yourself, ask, "Where does the 'I' reside?" Does it reside in the local self that receives a higher voice, or does it reside in the higher voice that communicates to the local selves? If you are residing in the local personality self, when you feel ready, deliberately shift your attention into the Beloved. Practice placing the "I" of your identity— the locus of your deepest sense of where the "I" resides as the Beloved. Recognize the feedback signals of joy, peace, love, and freedom as signs that you have made the inner shift. See how long you can hold these feelings until they become not a fleeting moment of grace but a state of being, even a "station," as Almaas calls it. Recognize these qualities as the Essence of yourself rather than a passing feeling.

Affirmations

Create your own affirmations, use them in your meditative time in the Inner Sanctuary, and repeat them throughout the day. Whenever your thoughts veer downward toward an old problem, worrying a wound aimlessly, consciously shift your attention to the affirmation. Let the affirmations become your mantras and experience incarnating these qualities in your being. Feel your Essential Self incarnating and integrating with your local self. For example:

> *I am* love.
> *I am* wisdom.
> *I am* faith.
> *I am* courage.
> *I am* power.
> *I am* patience.
> *I am* surrender.
> *I am* the Beloved.

Maintain the Self-Remembering Presence

Get used to the "is-ness" of yourself as the Beloved. Place your attention in that Essential Self, resting there in calmness as you go through your day. Sometimes it feels to me like an inner smile radiating out, warming myself, and all who pass by. It is the kind of smile you see on the face of the Dalai Lama, who is at peace despite the challenging circumstances he faces. He practices "initiatory love." His is not the kind of love you give when someone loves you, but the love you initiate from your own Essence unconditionally, because that is who you are as a Universal Human.

Speak Out Loud as the Beloved

To get started, it is very helpful to record your own inner voice, the "Voice of the Beloved." Practice writing in your journal as the Beloved, then reading what you write into a recorder. Place classical or baroque music behind it, like Pachelbel's "Canon in D." This tempo facilitates superlearning and memory.

Turn on your own recorded inner voice as you are going to sleep. When the voice of the Beloved speaks out loud in the household of selves, the cells awaken to their next phase of life. This is the signal they need to begin their cycle of regeneration and full expression of latent capacities.

Our cells are like seeds in spring, awaiting the warmth of the sun and the moisture of the rain. That sun and rain pour forth from the voice of the Beloved. Let it be heard in the land of your selves. The alchemical process of metamorphosis is accelerated through the vibration of the voice of the Beloved. Behold! We are experiencing a mystery, and we are being changed now.

Speak as Your Essential Self with Others

Speak as the Beloved, through inner dialogue or through conversation with others. This is a new form of conversation for emerging Universal Humans. The voice of the Beloved needs now to be spoken with one another. This creates a magnetic field of resonance between the two or more. The voice tone of each person stimulates the inner knowing of the others. Thoughts come forth that are deeper than the intellectual, analytical kind. They are thoughts resonant with direct knowing. They are like poetry and scripture coming from within us.

If at all possible, record these conversations and listen to them again and again. The combination of journaling, focused attention, inner-voice dialogues, and speaking out loud as the Beloved helps to secure the state of grace.

Meditation

You have come a long distance in your Emergence Process, and it may be helpful to recapture the entire process through a meditation that touches all previous steps. The following is one you may want to record and play back for meditation, if you find it useful:

I enter the Inner Sanctuary that resides forever in my being. I am at peace, I am at rest, I am fully protected and safe. In this sacred space, I place my attention on the Beloved that I am, dwelling in that brilliance and beauty of the presence of the Beloved, experiencing the qualities that I most particularly choose to express today.

I remember my invitation to the Beloved to take full dominion within the household of the separated selves. I remember the experience of that incarnation as the Beloved entering in at my invitation, infusing every fiber of my being with its divine radiance. I experience the Bliss of Union of the Human and the Divine.

I enter this field now, allowing the radiance to penetrate every cell and molecule of my being, as I feel myself disappear in the radiant field, losing all my boundaries of separation. I release my egoic separate identity, becoming one with the Beloved. In that oneness, I am one with all. I am infused with this bliss of union. My cells remember the pattern of their own regeneration and life ever more abundant.

I remain in the Inner Sanctuary for as long as my heart desires. When I am ready, I reappear, no longer a separated self. I am the eyes and ears and hands and feet of the Beloved. I am a Universal Human. I have come home now.

Journal

What does it feel like to make the shift from Infancy to Childhood, to form a new identity with your Essential Self fully integrated with your local self? As best you can, write as this new identity. Allow the voice to write as itself. Do not edit or think.

Describe what it feels like to shift the "I" of identity from the one who is asking to the one who knows. Note any changes in your vibrational field, your felt sense and inner experience of yourself. What are the feedback signals, perhaps feelings of joy, peace, love and a new sense of freedom, as you are making this inner shift?

As you write, experience how "the word becomes flesh." What is your experience of being the eyes, ears, hands and feet of the Beloved? You are not channeling a higher entity. You are the higher entity yourself.

Write your own set of declarative statements. Here are some of the ones that came through me. "I am the Guide who's been guiding. I am the voice I've been hearing. I am the Beloved that I have loved. I am the Universal Human I've been preparing to birth. As that I am here, present now, in every cell of my being." Write in your journal as the voice of this new identity as a young Universal Human.

Create and write your own affirmations. Let them become your mantras. Speak out loud as the voice of your Essential Self.

How are you giving expression to this new integrated identity in your life? In what new ways are you emerging? In what ways are you more receptive to the deeper patterns of creation?

Make a special section of your journal or use quotation marks to highlight the voice of the Beloved. Experiment with recording and sharing these written insights with others. They are your "inner scripture."

STEP SEVEN
Transferring Authority

As a child matures beyond infancy, it can no longer react in a totally self-centered way. It must learn to behave in the world, to follow its parents' and teachers' guidance. The young Universal Human does the same, but in the Emergence Process we learn that the parental authority is within us, as our essential divine Essence.

Until recently, the Beloved has remained aloof, signaling but not fully incarnating. The local selves were often left on their own, like latchkey children, trying to serve the higher purpose, but disconnected from their source of power, or acting without the intimate, felt presence of a loving parent. Now, as the process of incarnating continues, the Essential Self becomes proactive and is willing to be the genuine authority within the household of selves. This inner authority does not impose any form of punishment, guilt, or asceticism, for our local selves are becoming willing disciples of the Essential Self within.

The Story . . .

As I began to take authority as the Beloved, my local self let me know it didn't trust me to be fully present. In the past, I'd hovered and signaled from afar, leaving my local self on its own to complete the job without the advantage of my full presence and incarnation.

Local self had been put up to huge tasks through inspiring signals, such as "Go tell the story of the birth of a Universal Humanity," or "Work for the transformation of the American presidency" (which I did in 1984 by running and succeeding to have my name placed in nomination for the vice president of the United States on the Democratic ticket).

But I, as the Beloved, had not been fully incarnated. I had left the local selves to carry the burden of my commands given from afar without the energy and love that I infuse in them with my full radiant presence. My local selves suffered from the illusion of separation from me, which was the source of their anxiety and driven behavior.

This acceptance of inner responsibility and authority on the part of the Essential Self was clearly the next part of my process to experience the full power that I am. As I entered this stage, I had shifted my identity from local to Essential Self and was ready to transfer authority from the local selves who prod and push to the Beloved who literally takes the "throne" in the kingdom of heaven within. I realized that my external work in the world must now spring from the internal seat of authority, from the power of the Essential Self.

However, in the process, I discovered I didn't have a strong internal authority. My own inner parents needed maturing. In life, I'd had an overly dominant, demanding, very competitive, and successful father and a beautiful but submissive mother, underdeveloped because she had died so young. Within me, these two archetypes, my masculine and feminine aspects, were divided and immature, undermining my internal authority.

My father was irritable and brilliant, shouting at his employees, frightening his children and wife. I can still feel his personality acting out through me whenever I am flooded with irritation. But I learned to hate authority because of how my father used it and as a result have always resisted becoming the head of anything, not wanting the responsibility.

To strengthen my inner masculine, I envisioned the father I wish I'd had as being within myself. He listens carefully to my fears and desires. He has worldly wisdom and can take my hand and show a better way to achieve my heart's desire. He is powerful, creative, and infuses me with the energy of the inner masculine.

My feminine aspect also began to take shape. My own mother had never had a chance to mature, dying at thirty-three of breast cancer. I remember her as exquisitely beautiful, smiling shyly while my father ranted and raged, often in jest or love, but like a great bear in contrast to a gazelle. When I asked her in my prayers many years later, "Why did you die?" the answer I received was "I was so angry at your father, but I couldn't express myself, so I died."

My inner mother was arrested in her development and had never grown and matured. I in my own life had failed to be the nurturer to myself.

I started to bring forth the inner mother. I asked myself, Could I have a garden again? Could I open my recipe books, which I hadn't looked at for years? Could I simply enjoy myself in my home? Could I even have a home? I'd lost that side of my life.

I began to pay attention to the grieving girl within me who was motherless, always subtly seeking her mother in the most inappropriate people! I called her up unto me as the Divine Daughter. I embraced and nurtured her with all the mother love for which I had so yearned. I noticed that my chronic feeling of loneliness began to disappear.

When I returned home in the evening alone, instead of having that sinking feeling that harkened back to my feelings as a teenager, after my mother had died and I came home to an empty house, I actually looked forward to the time alone to be with my self! The sadness of loneliness became the pleasure of aloneness.

As I accepted the nurturing feminine side of myself, I began to experience the wise father, my masculine aspect, take firmer hold. I felt into the father's strength, creativity, entrepreneurial genius, buoyancy. I called the father to come home.

There was a new order in the household of wayward and lonely selves. The "locals" loved the presence of the matured mother/father and learned to "obey" with pleasure, for it truly felt better to be part of this orderly and loving inner home than wandering like lost children crying in the night. Mysteriously, when I honored and matured my inner parents rather than avoiding or escaping from them, they came together as one. When the mother and father are one, there the Essential Self is, and genuine Essential Self governance arises.

Now, I experience a joined masculine/feminine within me, and I draw on a fused Essence of mother/father as a co-creator. They no longer are jousting for control and domination but rest in true partnership within me. This is the "inner partnership" model. The gender differences have faded into wholeness. I am embodied as a woman, but when I am the Essential Self, I feel so complete that I don't actually notice feminine or masculine differences. The yin and the yang join to form a whole being.

I recorded the transition in my journal:

This morning I claimed inner authority and self-governance. I am the Beloved and speak with the authority as the Beloved, with the concerns of my local selves released and transformed into helpful signals about what needs to be done, with no negative charge within me. I can speak from my heart with the authority that is required as my work in the world unfolds.

It is vital in here that the local selves respond and adore the Beloved so that they can be absorbed, disappear and reappear as the Beloved on Earth calling forth the Essential Self in others.

When the local selves are in communion with me, experiencing their own absorption into me, I protect them from their tendency to separate from me. Just as worshippers in a church need to be protected in a sacred space from their own daily mundane concerns, so the worshipping local selves need to be protected by me from their mundane concerns. The local selves do not leave the sacred space to go "back" into the so-called real world. They are one with me, and together we go forward as the Universal Human.

Once I claimed authority within myself, the work of inner observation, of dialoguing between the local selves and the Beloved, became an active, continuous process. My walks in the morning after meditation and journal writing became a time of active inner dialogue. I invited a troubling local self to speak out loud, to say "I'm really upset about so-and-so." Then Beloved would respond with wisdom and love.

Whatever comes up, from a trivial irritation to a major crisis such as ill health, loss of a loved one, financial insecurity, natural disasters, is grist for the mill. If you have a true evolutionary perspective and you see that crises precede transformation, that problems are evolutionary drivers, then no matter what the challenge you are facing, you look first for what may be emerging, what more is being called forth from you. It is essential in these times to develop the inner authority such that you can turn inward for guidance and strength and become a wise and loving authority in dealing with the problem.

I have found that the joy of my life now is the unfolding of myself and others as that Essential Self, in a continuous process of self-discovery, self-observation, and communion with others doing the same.

In that context, I offer some points of guidance for this stage of development.

The Guidance . . .

We are now ready, as the new integrated identity, the young Universal Human, to accept full authority within ourselves. (The root of the word *authority* is the Latin *auctor,* meaning *creator*). We have been used to exerting external power over others as an egoic self or submitting to some external authority for direction in life. But at this step, we move toward what Gary Zukav, in his book *The Seat of the Soul* (1990), calls "authentic power," by which he means a power that flows from the Essential Self and leads to power from within—true empowerment of self and others.

At this step, the process of Emergence is comparable to the path of an astronaut. To be selected as an astronaut, one has to display qualities of excellence in all domains—temperament, intelligence, health, and relationships.

The same demands hold true of our Emergence as Universal Humans at this stage of our process. But unlike the astronauts, we have no external mission control, no external authority we can follow and depend upon. We have the control or guidance from within ourselves, as well as from wise and beloved others.

We may also draw upon the collective experience of a community of peers undergoing the same process as ourselves, but at the heart of it, there is no substitute for cultivating deep inner authority at the level of our own Essential Self.

In order for the transfer of power to take place, both the Essential Self and local selves must accept a deeper level of responsibility and discipline than ever before. The Essential Self needs to be present and responsible, and the local selves need to give up any remaining desire to act as separated selves. Without this, local selves will infuse the body/mind with their anxiety and prevent the Essential Self from operating.

This is yet another step in the process of the descent of the Beloved and ascent of the local self to join as one, coming into expression as the Universal Human. The local self must come to believe in the Essential Self's reality and must trust that self to be the source of all it seeks in the world. Almaas points out in *Essence* that ego won't let go until it is assured that everything is in place:

> Personality is not going to clear the space completely before it is sure that everything is covered. On the surface it appears that personality wants to displace essence. This is partially true, but on the deeper levels, it was formed and developed ultimately for protection. As essence is discovered, it is easier to let the personality go.

To go the whole way in the Emergence Process, the Essential Self within each of us must gain the trust of the local selves by agreeing to take full responsibility for their behavior and attitudes. This is not power over, but power from within.

As the Essential Self gains authority within the household, it learns to give loving, firm guidance and takes full dominion. The local selves begin to look up to Essential Self for guidance, like children look to the mother when they are confused or angry. Why would they want to follow anyone but her? She has the wisdom, she has the guidance, she offers the love that "passeth all understanding."

As the Essential Self assumes operational authority within the household of local selves, we are naturally led to mature our own inner parents, the often undeveloped masculine and feminine aspects of ourselves. The local selves look to the Beloved to have the qualities that ideally our real parents might have had but rarely did.

So many of us came from families that were dysfunctional, headed by parents who did not have a clue about their own or their children's self-development. Now, with the transfer of authority, we are becoming parents to ourselves at a deeper level, actually self-parenting ourselves from within. We must learn to do this job maturely, or there will be rebellion in the inner family, and the local selves will refuse to obey.

In this process of mature self-parenting, addictions and unresolved habitual patterns will come up and must be dealt with. These patterns are often deep and require power and understanding on the part of the inner authority to release them from their self-destructive behavior (as well as help from professional therapists where necessary).

Journal

Examine and write about your attitude toward authority in your life. Have you resented it in others? Have you exerted it over others? Do you approve of the way you handle authority now? Is your sense of internal authority weak or firm?

Review your attitude toward your mother and father, and imagine them matured, as you would like them to be. Then internalize these evolved parental figures, making them your own. Imagine them as being within yourself. Write as the matured, ideal parents you didn't have and begin to re-parent your wounded children, your local selves.

How does this bring into a new balance the masculine and feminine aspects of your being?
How do you experience the transfer of authority to your Essential Self? Are there ways in which you have gained greater "authentic power"? Are there troubling patterns that arise? As your own Inner Authority, how can you reassure your local selves and gain their trust? You will learn more about how to deal with persistently troubled local selves in the next step.

Educating the Local Selves

True education of the local selves by the Essential Self begins when we are no longer looking outward to external principalities and powers but are experiencing the Bliss of Union, the Shift of Identity, and the Transfer of Authority as an ongoing, ever-deepening process. It continues as we are willing to learn response-ability for our own Emergence and fulfillment as Universal Humans. We are no longer victims. There is no one to blame. We become co-creators of our own reality, entering an inspired dance between the local selves, the Essential Self, other people, and the larger field, which is informing us all. The choreographer of this divine dance is the universal Designing Intelligence incarnating in and as us.

The Story . . .

I have been involved in the process of Emergence for many years now. It has taken patience, self-compassion, and a continual return to bliss. I am amazed at the personal rewards I am receiving. I am freeing myself from chronic anxiety, compulsion, and fear of failure. I have learned to reside at the still, quiet center of my being and experience the presence of the Beloved as myself most of the time.

The work I've been doing in the world is taking hold in a new way. It is this process of Emergence, still unfolding within me, that I want to offer to all who so desire.

I am enlarging the Inner Sanctuary to include a "Sunlit Garden of Co-creation." This is an expanding place in the larger world, still protected, like a sacred garden, where I can meet and co-create with others in real life; for example, in my office next to my computer, I have flowers and often pictures of my beloveds. When I meet with a co-worker, I try to remember to stop for a moment, breathe together, check in with each other, and develop our work from the deeper source of our being.

Because I am not yet fully stabilized, my local selves may be bombarding me with questions and demands, each one pulling me, the Beloved, momentarily out of the Garden. I, the Beloved, or Essential Self, am still challenged to assume full authority within the household of my selves.

I am gaining the full radiant power to actually calm the local selves when they are attempting to solve problems in separation from me. I am achieving a sustainable, steady state of integrated ego/Essence. As I am normalizing this state, my local selves are better able to stay connected with Essence in the Sunlit Garden. I am learning to do my work as an ex- pression of my essential being. Through this Emergence Process, I am experiencing ever more deeply the "pearl beyond price"—that unique Essence I am as a Universal Human.

The instant I am aware of a separating, judgmental thought arising, I quickly lift the local, grieving self into the Sunlit Garden. If she is deeply distressed, I take her into the Inner Sanctuary where she fuses with the divine once again. Then we move outward into the Sunlit Garden from the inner to the outer world. There, the local self remembers its heart's desire is already met. It is content and at home. When ego and Essence fuse, relaxation deepens. As the stress of separation disappears, the Bliss of Union spreads. The pleasure centers in the brain flood the system with happiness.

As my local selves are educated, they become willing instruments of my unfolding. My local selves continue to act up, but now that more is happening in my work in the world, I am entering the Sunlit Garden as a continuing practice, doing my work as an expression of integrated ego/Essence. I am developing the practice of creating "heaven" in myself and hopefully in others as we join to do our life's work. We are learning the process of co-creation.

I am freeing myself from the gut-level pains that were part of my driven separate self. I often do an emotional internal scan to see if there's any pain left.

For example, a chronic impatience with the pace of my work, irritation, and frustration used to flood my nervous system on a daily basis, no matter how hard I worked. Now, instead of letting it override and run me, or trying to ignore or deny it, I penetrate the depth of the feeling. It's a feeling of urgency—"I'll never finish my work!"—or even worse, "The world is running out of time. We won't make it."

Probing the impatience uncovers a hornet's nest. I penetrate all the way down to the depths, where the self has first felt its separation from God. There, I find the root of this illusory separation, the hopeless feeling that I, egoic self, have to make the world transform. I stop, and because I have been practicing in the Inner Sanctuary, I surrender into the bliss of union. I consciously lift the impatience up into the field of bliss. There, the world is already transformed, and I, the Beloved, am already "there." The goal of my chronic impatience, to do the job of creating a new world, was in truth already fulfilled, right now, by the experience of being at peace internally. Coming from this inner experience, I am more likely to be a positive influence on the healing of the world!

I wrote in my journal:

> *In this Sunlit Garden, I, the Beloved, establish this blessed school where the young Universal Human learns to grow up. In this sunny expanded Sanctuary, I bring up unto me all disconnected local selves trying inadequately to handle problems. I say to all of them, "Come up unto me. I will take your burdens, I will heal your pain. Stop trying to figure anything out or solve anything in this agitated state.*

"Nothing you attempt from your separated state will work. You are off duty now! You are to come up higher, past all your local self contractions, into the field of lightness, joy, wisdom, and empowerment through resonance with Me, through attunement with the larger design and the actual truth of each situation.

"I who before have been abstract and discarnate, must truly exercise my presence and authority to create the heaven within where the local selves can meet with me in absolute safety.

"In this divine arena of integration and infusion, I exercise for the first time my full authority, love, and wisdom within this household.

"It is my place of learning to be fully incarnated, holding the love and intention for all my local selves, as a teacher does with disciples.

"My local selves are my disciples. I am the teacher within. Now it is my turn to learn to teach, to presence myself with such radiance and attraction that all my local selves are magnetized toward me.

"This is the way I create 'Heaven on Earth.'"

The Guidance . . .

In order to accomplish the education of the local selves, we consciously create an expanded space, the Sunlit Garden of Co-creation, a place in consciousness of joy, safety, beauty, and love, where the separated selves join the divine and become educated in the power of co-creation. This is like a kindergarten for children. As young Universal Humans, we are placing ourselves in such a protected space of learning.

In this Garden, the Beloved resides permanently. It is its domain, and it radiates unconditional love, sitting upon the seat of authority in the kingdom of heaven within. The Essential Self invites the household of local selves to enter, calling them to freedom from the pain of separation, from the addiction to their strategies that are not working any longer.

The local selves flock to the Beloved eagerly, freely, and voluntarily giving up their pursuit of happiness in separation. In its presence they are released from bondage to their pain of separation, to their unfulfilled ambitions, their sense of failure, and lack of self-worth. The Beloved is fulfilling their heart's desire. A magnetic attraction pulls the "disciples" toward it. They are willing to commit to the self-discipline required for full integration with the Essential Self.

The adoring local selves energize the Essential Self. We experience new empowered capacities—Essential Self presencing, Essential Self radiating, Essential Self impressing—which deepen and strengthen as the local selves focus attention on the Beloved, enabling it to come into full force within us.

In this vibrational field of devotion, the egoic selves are fully relaxed and attentive. They want to be with the Beloved, indeed, to be consummated through union with it much like the mystic's passion for union with God. Only this passion turns inward toward the God-self, the unique and personal Essence of the divine.

To educate our local selves, we must deal with their various aspects: the good local selves, the anxious local selves, the distressed local selves. We also must deal with the deeper problem from which all local selves spring, the illusion of our separation from God and each other. We focus on practices, which train our local selves and lead to our full Emergence as Universal Humans.

The milieu in which this education best takes place is an expanded state of bliss, a true culture of ecstasy. The local selves absorb the vibrational field of the Beloved such that the alchemical process is accelerated within them. In order for this to happen, discipline is required, but not the discipline of rewards and punishment. There is no force or compulsion here. It's the discipline of actually experiencing yourself as you are, which is ecstatic.

In the Garden, the course of studies offered is everything the local selves could possibly desire: the Bliss of Union, the promise of the fusion of genius, the explosion of their creativity, the ecstasy of co-creation—the full incarnation as divinity. Joy. Gladness. Heaven on Earth within us! Who would turn this down if they knew its fabulous rewards?

One of our first tasks is to practice freeing ourselves from all pressure of time—the local self's compulsion to "get the job done" before time runs out. We have dealt with the pressure of time in the Inner Sanctuary, but now we practice under the guidance of our Essential Self as authority.

Here we learn to move from local, linear time (the domain of local self) to nonlocal, nonlinear time, the pure experience of the present (the domain of Essential Self). In this process, the local selves realize that of themselves they can do nothing. The Father/Mother, the Great Creating Process, "doeth the work." We come to realize that this inner union is the job that needs to get done to transform anything in oneself and the world. This is the fundamental work, which will best serve the world.

Freedom from the urgency of time releases the local selves, allowing them to be absorbed in the vibrational field of the Beloved's ever-present Now. In this field, the local self's problems and issues are dissolved, not solved. When we shift our attention down to the level of the problems we are trying to solve, we descend in our vibration. From this vantage point, we feel separate and cannot solve our problems. But once the local selves are lifted up into the love field of the Beloved, their stress is released, their patterns are dissolved, and in that divine milieu, the Beloved can point out the truth of the situation to the local selves.

In this process, we learn to create a new center of gravity in ourselves. Instead of our local self's thoughts and concerns drawing Beloved's attention downward, contaminating the nervous system with stress, we create a new and stronger thought field of attraction. This field magnetizes wayward thoughts before they impact the nervous system. If we can learn to take a negative thought up quickly, before it enters our nervous system, we will not be affected by the thought. This is self-evolution through self-elevation.

However, if certain patterns of worry, blame, or impatience persist, seeming to resist being repatterned in the field, we may need to deal with them more directly. I have found the technique described by Almaas in his Diamond Approach helpful and have adopted it in my inner work when a local self issue chronically reoccurs, even after being lifted up.

Almaas (*Essence*) suggests we directly experience the deficiencies of the ego or local self and recognize that what the ego is attempting to get is already present in Essence. The process here is to feel deeply ego's lack, or "hole," as Almaas calls it, and not defend against this feeling of lack, nor come up with any strategies for solving the problem from the egoic point of view.

It is a two-step process: First, the Beloved invites the local selves to come forward to describe as deeply as possible any pain or deficiency being experienced—the needs, wants, pain. We don't defend against the feeling, don't try to fix or solve it from the egoic point of view, but rather completely allow it to be present and fully feel it—its location in the body, its density, vibration. Second, we stay with that pain and follow it all the way to the root, the source where we first felt such pain.

According to Almaas, when we follow the deficiency as deeply as possible, it leads us to that part of Essence or the Beloved that the local self has been seeking by trying to have some strategy in the outer world. In other words, we let our local selves discover that the fulfillment they've been seeking is already present in the Beloved. Ego becomes the guide to Essence.

Almaas describes the process in *Essence:*

> When one allows oneself quietly to experience the hurtful wound and memories connected with it, the golden elixir will flow out of it, healing it, and filling the emptiness with the beautiful sweet fullness that will melt the heart, erase the mind, and bring about the contentment that the individual has been thirsting for. . . . Ego's search for satisfaction being over, because you're not defending, not strategizing, leads you to that part of the Pearl that it's been seeking by strategizing.

When the problem is brought up into the domain of the Essence, the Essence with probing intelligence, helps the local self see that the source of the problem is its own illusion of separation. It reveals that the Beloved within holds the very qualities the local self was seeking outside.

In the field of resonance, the ego experiences a reunion with Essence, and the pain disappears. The local self releases its sense of judgment on itself and others. It stops trying to negotiate and be right and experiences compassion for itself and others, taking on the vantage of the Beloved toward itself. The local selves become wise enough to see themselves through the eyes of their own divinity. From this view, there is no right and wrong, no good and no evil, only truth, and the truth sets us free of judgment.

In the resonant field, local self distress is unstressed. Egoic problems are not in the first instant solved. They are dissolved. In the resonant vibrational field of the divine Essence, problems fade and no longer seem to exist. As our local selves are educated, they begin to become the instruments of our unfolding.

We discover that underneath all specific symptoms, which feel so personal and unique, there is usually one fundamental source from which the particular problem springs. That is ego's separation from Essence, or in traditional language, the human separation from God. Therefore, the fundamental solution to many of our problems is the union of ego and Essence on a collective scale. Most of our major problems are caused by social structures of top down, dominance, and control where the collective ego is in charge! As each of us shifts our identity from ego to Essence, we are making a significant contribution toward both personal and social transformation.

Bringing the Inner Sunlit Garden of Co-creation Out into the World

While you are in the Inner Sanctuary, even as you lie in bed half awake, invite your local selves to be with you in complete seclusion, where they have absolutely nothing to do and nowhere to go. Then begin to imagine being in the

Sunlit Garden of Co-creation. Allow your imagination to reveal to you the most important work you can do that day. This practice can offer to you a moment of revelation of your deeper life's purpose and how to fulfill it through your work that very day.

Once you establish this Sunlit Garden while still resting in the Inner Sanctuary, you can better move outward into the day with continuity of Essential Self awareness. You will stay more securely connected to the vibrational field of your integrated ego/Essence as you do your work in the world.

You will find that throughout the day you reside in the Garden. Mundane events are infused with the presence of the Beloved. You realize that your life itself is being transformed. You become more clearly the cause of your own experience rather than at the effect of it. You are a co-creator and become a beneficent presence through your work in the world.

Let Ego Guide You to Essence

Practice the Almaas technique by focusing on your "holes," or deficiencies, presented to you by the local self. Select some aspect of your being that feels pain or is grieving, lacking in something. In the Sunlit Garden, take time to focus on the deficiency. Feel it as deeply as possible for as long as needed. Be completely open, with no thoughts of how to "fix it" or make it better.

Just let it be fully, whatever it is, with no resistance whatsoever. Then wait, as Almaas suggests, for ego to guide you precisely to the quality within yourself that you have been seeking. Ego becomes your guide to Essence. Then, contemplate, cultivate, love that quality in your Essential Self that ego has been fruitlessly seeking. Be present as that quality. Let it sink in. In this way, you "metabolize" your ego. Ego is consumed in the alchemical furnace of Essence, the great transformer within.

Use your inner authority to set up the conditions for ego to bring forth the very qualities of Essence that you seek. Even one success in this process will encourage you to do more. For example, when I let the grieving girl guide me to the mother she had sought, I was then convinced that I could heal any aspect of my personality. The Essential Self always knows the next step needed for our own healing. We can rest assured that the teacher within truly knows everything we need to know.

Acknowledge the Good in Most Local Self Motivation

Underneath the stress of the local self's efforts to succeed, to win self-esteem, and to prevail in the world is a deeper motivation. That motivation is often good but misguided. Ego is working for your safety and success in the world. Once it is incorporated into the Beloved, the ego reappears as the executive capacities of your whole being to bring your Essence into form in the world. Thank the local selves for their devotion to their purpose of protecting you. Once the Beloved is actually in charge, the good motivation of local selves has been fulfilled. They are ready to release their illusions and compulsions.

Do unto Others' Local Selves What You Do for Your Own

To the degree that we can guide our own local selves, we can be compassionate and helpful to another's egoic personality. When we learn not to judge our own egoic personality, we are far less judgmental of others. As we learn to presence ourselves as the Beloved, we can transmit the energy of the Beloved to the Beloved in others. This transmission awakens the inner presence in other people, and they begin to access their own inner Essential Self. They are lifted up by your presence.

Firmly Close the Door

It may be true that local selves no longer want to escape into addictive patterns, yet the patterns of separation are extremely deep and persistent. It helps here, once again, to close the door with a definitive internal gesture of finality. Here are some suggested affirmations, and feel free to write your own.

This is the end of separation. I have crossed the great divide. I will not go back again. I may be young, but I am born. I will never return to the illusion of separation.

This set of clear affirmations trains local selves not to revert to old patterns of escape and ego-driven compulsions.

Be Alert to the Recurrence of Chronic Anxiety

Develop a sensitive biofeedback system to alert you to anxiety. The instant you feel anxious, stop and do not let it override you. Anxiety means an aspect of the local self has taken charge in the household of selves. The Beloved, now the inner authority, needs to respond quickly, just like a parent would to a child who is about to fall down and hurt itself. Use whatever technique works for you to return to center. There are many ways as there are individuals. Invent your own.

Journal

In order to educate any wayward local selves, imagine a Sunlit Garden of Co-creation, an extension of the Inner Sanctuary. It is a protected place of learning integration where the Beloved radiates unconditional love and healing energy toward the local selves. Describe this Sunlit Garden in your journal. Be playful and creative.

If there is a part of you, a local self that persists in feeling pain and anxiety, carefully review the Almaas process described above. Take time to focus on this aspect of your being that feels a deficiency or "hole." Be completely open to its feelings without resistance.

Give voice to its concerns in its own words by writing them in your journal as if this hurting local self is speaking directly to the Beloved.

What does the Beloved have to say in response? Record any dialogue or interactions between the two.

Allow your ego to guide you to the quality within yourself that it has been seeking. Let your ego become your guide to Essence. Then be fully present to that quality. Describe and savor the qualities of your Essential Self that ego has been fruitlessly seeking. As you write let them sink in and incorporate them fully into your being.

Keep writing in your journal as you receive guidance. This is precious information. Keep a record of your progress in dealing with things that are persistently difficult for you.

Meditation

Locate within your heart a point of pure white light,
the open space within you where Spirit pours forth
its radiance, animating and informing your Essence.
It is the place where universal creativity infuses
your Essential Self with the radiant presence of the
divine. Feel the entire process of creation that ani-

mates all being focused in your heart as your own impulse of Emergence.

Place your consciousness in this center. It is your direct contact with Source. Let this universal presence infuse your Essential Self with white light. Your Beloved Self is now fusing with Source. You are one with the universal mind of God. Then expand gently outward into the Rose Chamber of Union of the Human and the Divine. Place your identity in the Beloved, feeling its radiance and warmth.

Invite all your local selves to enter into union with you as the Beloved. Let the weary and wounded egoic selves enter into the Inner Sanctuary. Radiate your divine vibration upon them. Dissolve their density. Release their contractions. Entrain them in your vibrational field until they are consumed in your radiance, and vibrate at the frequency of the Beloved. Feel all your local selves fuse with you.

Experience the bliss of union.

Now open the sacred environment of the Inner Sanctuary to the Sunlit Garden of Co-creation where other young Universal Humans play. Let the matured local selves enter the garden together. It is filled with flowers, scents, sights, tastes, sounds, and beauty that delight and charm the local selves. It is a place of play, a kindergarten of godlings.

Visualize masters of the past and present looking on benignly, supervising at a distance. Bring forth your most beloved spiritual teachers and ancestors. Allow them to be with you, to bless and embrace you in joy at your appearance among them. They have been waiting for your arrival for a long time. Let them infuse you with their Essence and the qualities of being you most desire. Ask that those qualities be incarnate in you. Feel each of them blessing you. Affirm their presence as you acknowledge your own Emergence.

Experience your communion with the divine beings who have gone before and are paving the way for your Emergence. Luxuriate and play in the Inner School for Conscious Evolution.

STEP NINE

The Repatterning of Life

At this final step in our Childhood, we ripen and come to a new level of maturity in our development as Universal Humans. Just as a child attending school for the first time is awkward and then gradually gains confidence, so are we, as young Universal Humans, gradually coming into a greater Essential Self confidence, a deeper trust of our inner knowing, a new way of relating to one another. We are at home in the kindergarten of the godlings.

At this step, the more we let go of egoic fears, the more we find that our external life reflects the deeper guidance and motivation of the Essential Self. There is a coincidental relationship between inner integration and outer manifestation. We see clear demonstration that the inner creates the outer, that intention manifests, that our consciousness is causal in the events, relationships, projects, and visions of our lives.

The Story . . .

As the Emergence Process accelerated within me, I found myself trying to hold on to my old pattern out of fear that I would be left bereft. I clung to my familiar life pattern, knowing that it was not working as it was, especially in my work and my relationship. But I was afraid to let go.

Despite my fearful efforts to maintain it, the old pattern disintegrated and fell away. This is natural. The old social structures that sustained us are breaking down, while new consciousness and social systems are barely breaking through. Few of us have yet found where we fit best in the emerging world. The structures in our personal life often can no longer support us as they did. We may have new vocations, callings, yet there are few experts, no labels, and no pay! We are pioneers. Feelings of fear, chaos, and panic, both in our inner world as well as the outer world, are natural and real. Yet, when we see our problems from an evolutionary perspective, we recognize that our crisis is potentially the birth of a new culture and a new human. From the vantage point of our Essential Self, we realize that such problems and concerns are evolutionary drivers. They are stimulating our own Emergence.

Nonetheless, during this period I went through a period of panic. Chaos seemed to be everywhere. It felt like "failure," but in retrospect I see that, as is so often the case, the breakdown was absolutely essential to allow the breakthrough to occur.

When I have shared this story with other evolutionary leaders, I find that they are experiencing the same phenomenon. Yet most of us find that when we persevere in our inner growth and in our vocational callings, in humility, faith, and good cheer, the process itself will often jump our life and work ahead into a new domain that fulfills our deepest heart's desire.

It is vital in the early days of our Emergence to follow that "compass of joy" through the darkness of our confusion. It will lead to fulfillment if we will only stay the course. This inner compass guides us when we discover and say *yes* to our deeper life purpose, to what attracts us to give. This *yes* is a sign that the impulse of evolution is guiding us. It resides in and as our Essential Selves.

The more chaotic it gets in your personal as well as social life, the more important it is to deepen your practice in the Inner Sanctuary and the Sunlit Garden of Co-creation. You will be able to stay connected on the inner plane as you move out into your daily life and work in the world. The more often you can share this process with others who are going through the same, the more you will stabilize.

I have found that my heart's deepest desire for a more full life, for higher consciousness and greater freedom, has never guided me falsely. I realize that this yearning is the direction of evolution itself, not just my own personal need. At every choice point, I followed the evolutionary signals from within toward more consciousness, greater freedom of expression, and more cooperative and co-creative relationships. This is the trajectory of billions of years of evolution encoded in each of us. When the Essential Self takes authority, this sense of direction is enhanced.

Through this developmental process we gain an "evolutionary faith" that our struggles are not just a personal whim or a sign of failure of ourselves or of society. They are in the great tradition of evolution itself. Crises precede transformation. Problems are evolutionary drivers. Nature takes jumps through greater synergy, separate people coming together to form new wholes greater than the sum of our parts. We are this story come alive. We are the universe in person!

This faith is alive in the Essential Self. It gives meaning to our crises and guidance to our new powers.

The daily journal writing intensified as "I," the Beloved, consciously wrote as the *"I am"* to my local selves:

> *I am calling you to the complete family reunion within Me. Bring the separated mind home to the God within. Through this fusion of selves within, we will come through the fire of alchemical transformation from our creature to our co-creative phase. Our will joins the universal design of creation—wholes within wholes within wholes.*
>
> *It is our teaching of this that will bring in everything we need as we need it.*
>
> *You, local selves, release your anxiety, and allow Me, who is one with the Great Creating Process, to lift you up unto the radiant, self-transcending process of creation out of which we are continuously being created.*
>
> *Local selves, in all your diversity and individuality, now release your burdens completely and enter the Holy of Holies, the Rose Chamber of Union of the Human and the Divine. Here you must dwell in blissful union every day during this vital period of repatterning. Oth-*

erwise, the alchemical process is aborted, the old anxiet-
ies flood your system, and you are set back further than
if you never began. This is a dangerous period. This is
the birth process of a new identity. And we don't have
full models of what we are becoming.

The Guidance . . .

This external repatterning of our lives can be difficult, not
what we may have expected. Dysfunctionalities, situations
that have not worked for years, aspects of our lives that are
out of alignment with our Essential Self, begin to show up.
They become intolerable in contrast with the new inner
harmony.

The dissonance at this more advanced stage can actually
abort the alchemical process and be more destructive than
dissonance was when we were more fully egoic. The contrast
is sharper and thus more painful, making it seem as though
everything is breaking down. But it is vital to the process that
this breakdown be allowed to proceed without fear.

If we can stay centered, relax, and "let go, let God,"
as the popular saying goes, we will find that dysfunctionalities begin to drop away, while on the other hand, new
"functionalities" appear. Things that seemed impossible to
manifest before now begin to happen effortlessly. "Miracles"
happen, but they are only miracles from the perspective of
the separated mind. From the point of view of the Beloved,
they are natural. At this stage, the willingness to tolerate

ambiguity and uncertainty is a prized quality for our continued Emergence.

When new order starts forming out of chaos in our own lives, we realize we too are part of the self-organizing universe that brought us from subatomic particles to this very instant of time. It is no more miraculous that we should evolve into a higher order than the fact that subatomic particles made atoms and that molecules made cells.

Everything is miraculous and mysterious beyond the understanding of the rational mind.

As we release our bondage to the separated self, we enter more deeply the organic unfolding of nature. We are in alignment with the deeper patterns that are creating all existence including us. After all, nature arose and is continuously arising out of an invisible, nonphysical field able to self-organize from nothing at all to everything that is, following a deep tendency toward higher consciousness and greater freedom through more complex order. We are expressions of that transcendent, awesome, magnificent, universal organizing intelligence.

When our separated minds quiet down, our deeper self, which is one with that intelligence, comes forth. We learn to sustain the internal resonance of our inner state as we work in the world. We learn to maintain resonance with others, doing the work together. In fact, being and doing blend together seamlessly.

We see this in nature. We do not look at a leaf and ask, "Is it being or doing?" It is simply being itself—leafing. When we are at one with the Essence of our being, we lose "self" consciousness. We are in the flow; we are the very Essence expressing itself.

If subatomic particles could make atoms, and atoms could make molecules, and molecules cells, and so on up the great spiral of evolution, then surely we can Self–organize to fulfill our own creative potential in cooperation with others doing the same. It is natural. What is unnatural is the illusion that we are separate from that cosmic intelligence that is creating everything that is.

Ken Wilber writes in *One Taste* (1999) how our Essence expresses in the process of creation:

> Once you find your formless identity as Buddha-mind, as Atman, as pure Spirit or Godhead, you will take that constant, non-dual, ever-present consciousness and reenter the lesser states . . . reanimate them with radiance. . . . You will pour yourself out into the mind and world, and create them in the process, and enter them all equally, but especially and particularly that specific mind and body that is called you. . . . You will then awaken as radical freedom, and sing those songs of radiant release, beam an infinity too obvious to see, and drink an ocean of delight. . . .

As we are shifting our attention and identity to the Essential Self and experience the world outside from this inner vantage point, the outer action seems miraculously to repattern itself to a higher order, one that is more resonant with our inner values. The steps we are to take in accomplishing our work are revealed spontaneously.

Ease of effort replaces overwhelm. Peace dissolves anxiety, panic, and nervousness. The external process flows from within and reflects the power and authority of the Essential Self. "As above, so below."

To stabilize yourself in day-to-day life as a young Universal Human requires deep perseverance, radical evolutionary faith, and the profoundly loving devotion of a parent for a child who wakes crying in the middle of the night. We are reparenting ourselves. We need to nurture our own Emergence Process, because as the Beloved, we are mothering and fathering, training the still-vulnerable and wayward local selves.

The following are some practices to support this process and some attitudes to adopt and cultivate as you mature in this phase of Childhood, beginning the transition into the Youth of the Universal Human.

Allow Your Life to Repattern

Shift from controlling your daily life through planning and organizing to include elements of discovery, appreciation, and resonance in all your activities. By letting go of control, you allow a new pattern to unfold. Be receptive to synergies, synchronicities, and attractions as they appear in your projects and relationships. Allow space for the visionary aspect of the Beloved to infuse you with inspiration. Cultivate the feeling of joy.

Self-Presencing

The best practice at this stage is to center yourself in the Beloved and remain calm at the core of the chaos, placing your intention into the field and allowing the organizing process to reveal the way. Practice feeling the Beloved as yourself, peaceful, all-knowing, fulfilled, always already present as the presence. Remember that you are the Beloved. The Essential Self knows and has guided you until this moment. Now you are that guide. You and It are one. Our faith makes us whole.

Realize That You Are Fully Response-able

You can respond to every need that arises. Affirm that, as the Beloved, you are not needy, afraid, or lonely. You are attracting every resource and person you need. You are entering the finest time of your life. You are ready to come into new form, informed by the process of creation itself.

Cultivate Resonance by Attuning with Others

In this early phase of repatterning, it is vital to draw others to you to create a field of resonance, a growth culture for the young Universal Human. The repatterning of our lives leads to co-creation, but it takes time. The formation of small resonant Emergence Circles—the two or more gathered—is vital at this stage. Do not try to do this alone. You need the "field." It is like mother's milk to the newly born Universal Human.

Nourish the Beloved

Create a special place in your meditation to simply be your Essential Self, without paying any attention to the needs and demands of local selves. We do not want to have a work-a-day Beloved, getting worn out by attending to needs of the local selves, like a mother with a colicky child. Take time for the Beloved to plug into the radiant, non-dual, infinite reality and dwell in its real home, which is God.

Journal

Write a description of what is falling away in your life and what is emerging that is new. How are breakdowns leading to personal breakthroughs. What are you learning from the challenges you are facing?

Describe how the inner "Compass of Joy" is guiding you through any darkness or confusion you may be experiencing. Describe the synchronicities and synergies that are arising into your life.

In what ways do you see yourself aligning with the deeper patterns of creation, the universal organizing intelligence?

Allow your deepest heart's desire for more life, for higher consciousness, and greater freedom to express itself fully. Describe the desire. Intend it. Affirm it. Declare it as already so. Realize that the "force of creation" is with you—as You!

YOUTH

STEP TEN
Fulfilling the Promise

We are crossing the threshold from our Childhood into the vast and as-yet-uncharted realm of our Youth as Universal Humans. We are undergoing a new rite of passage, yet to be fully acknowledged in this world. To prepare, we first cast our eye backward in time to see the exquisite pattern of our Emergence, guided silently and mysteriously by our Essential Selves.

We remember our conception and gestation, our first awakenings in the womb of self-consciousness, our resonance with spiritual ancestors and guides, our healings of the wounded aspects of the local self, our vocational arousal, our willingness to say yes to the incarnation of our Essential Self, our desire to co-create with others. We honor the definitive moment of recognition that our growth is no longer possible when driven by our egoic local self. We are born, sometimes gracefully, other times painfully, and we enter our Infancy where we contemplate the glory of the Beloved within.

Through our attention, we learn to magnetize the incarnation of the Higher Self; we invite the Essential Self to take dominion within the household of selves and experience the bliss of union with our divine Essence. From there, we enter our Childhood, shifting our identity from ego to Essence, transferring authority to the Beloved within, and beginning the lifelong process of educating our local selves and repatterning our lives.

At last, we arrive in the developmental path at a very early phase of Youth, ready now to come into form in the evolution of our selves and our world. We celebrate within us the shift from the creature human to the co-creator.

The Story . . .

The transition between Childhood and Youth, similar to the transition between Infancy and Childhood, is not marked by a sudden shift but by a gradual unfolding. Yet one day, I woke up and noticed that a very real phase change had taken place, a shift as definitive as that from prepuberty to puberty, or from menarche to menopause. I felt that I had graduated from Childhood. I now reside as the Essential Self and am ready to commit to action at a larger scale. This is the new hero's journey, and all emerging Universal Humans are on it.

As I enter Youth now, I am securing my identity in Essence rather than ego and am taking full responsibility for the household of my many and wayward local selves. It is clear that my life has been repatterned, as the outward manifestation more and more reflects the inner knowing.

We discover that we are part of a living social organism. All the work is interconnected. We are reaching out, connecting with partners, collaborative initiatives, and enterprises throughout the world.

Everything I have ever thought of is "coming true" in new form. I am constantly stretching, challenged to go beyond my past limits, getting newer every day.

Yet, in the midst of all this activity, I have finally come to realize that my "goal" is not any external activity, important as goals are, but rather myself emerged, stabilized, and whole as a new norm, in loving relationship with and in support of others doing the same.

For all my adult life, I have had a purpose in the world to "go tell the story of the birth of a Universal Humanity." Although my essential Self had signaled me for years to "create an aura of silence about you until you can hear me at all times . . . until your self-centered mind is fully incorporated in your God-centered mind," my local self often ignored the focus on the Beloved and continued to feel compelled to work in the world, overriding the deeper guidance for Essential Self–realization.

Now, in my Youth, having cultivated the Bliss of Union and the process of my own and others' Emergence for many years, I have finally followed this guidance and am experiencing the "rewards." Deepening and sharing this process of inner union, communion, and co-creating toward the larger planetary shift is the primary purpose of my mission on Earth. While it will take generations for the next phase of social evolution to unfold, it is also true that this experience is available within us now and is the wellspring out of which the new world is coming.

The shift of identity is quantum; that is, it jumps from one orbit to the next with no distance in between, like an electron. I don't have to get here. I am here. Then, once I am aware of that, I can unfold in time/space. And it is from this position, at the other side of the quantum jump, already here as the Universal Human, that we can best guide ourselves through this period of quantum transformation and radical newness.

As long as I was thinking that I had to fulfill some external goal as my primary purpose, I was prevented by that very striving from achieving the goal I was intending. I realize now that this integration of being/doing is vital to my social purpose. For only as this whole being can I fully express and manifest what I am called to do.

If I do what I do as one who is trying to reach a goal, that goal will forever recede from my grasp, and I will forever be grasping. However, if I am the goal, if the Universal Human incarnate is the goal right now, then I am forever liberated from seeking or grasping at anything, and my work will have a quality that truly serves others as it serves myself.

This is the first moment in my whole life in which I have ever felt that my purpose is being fulfilled. By accepting this state of wholeness as my purpose, I have taken a quantum leap.

As Almaas (*Essence*) says: "A person living in the present can have goals, but the goals are an expression and the result of who the person is at the moment. The person is already fulfilled and that fulfillment can then manifest as certain goals."

The Guidance . . .

What are the fruits of this new phase of being? How does it serve others? Being the Essential Self in person is an ultimate service to humanity, because then we transmit that Essence to others spontaneously, helping others to shift from ego to Essence by our presence.

Hold a Mirror for Others to See Who They Truly Are

We become mirrors in which others can see the "glory" of who they truly are. By holding a clear surface for others to see themselves as we see them, we mature ourselves as Universal Humans as we serve others. And as we make the shift from ego to Essence, we can better guide the larger society through its transition from collective egoic behavior, as expressed in vast military spending, nuclear proliferation, environmental destruction, and so on. We cannot transform the world as local selves, no matter how well motivated we are.

Access within Yourself an Expanded Guide, a More Profound Aspect of the Inner Beloved

We deliberately and gently expand the space of the Inner Sanctuary and the Sunlit Garden into our daily lives. We deepen the guidance of the Essential Self by consciously being in that state with others in our work. As we find the way to do more of what we feel called to do, the inner guidance of the Essential Self becomes clearer often in the moment. We may experience "higher mind," spontaneous knowing what to do, heightened intuition, deeper powers of communication, communion, and love of others.

Call upon this presence to provide the deeper wisdom you need to bring yourself out into the world into form that expresses your Essential Self.

Surrender the Figuring-It-Out Mind

The guidance for newness comes from the profound pattern of evolutionary design embedded in nature and in human nature. In the presence of our deepening wisdom, we surrender the figuring-it-out mind. We bring to waking consciousness the inner intuitive knowing, the gnosis, as a continual wise presence, as we are doing our daily work in the world through the agency of the local selves. We quiet the "waters of the mind" moment by moment, making of life itself an expression of Essence. This is a life art form to be developed by young Universal Humans. The mind remains poised, and the essential love/intelligence emerges in each instant. Life becomes a continual spiritual experience. We carry our Inner Sanctuary or temple with us wherever we go. Life and work become sacred expressions.

Have Compassion upon Yourself

We must have compassion upon ourselves. There is no society on this Earth, as far as we know, that has been through a planetary phase change from the high technology, over-populating, polluting phase to the next phase of universal co-creative evolution, which we are envisioning as our possible future. This macrocosmic "birth transition" is not taught in our great universities. There are no experts in planetary transformation, because no one has lived through it.

While there are many spiritual schools for the evolution of the person toward God realization, there are only a few places, as we have noted, just now emerging, where we learn to be co-creators of the next stage of self and social evolution.

As we learn to mature the inner parents to act as our guiding authority, so now we mature ourselves in our future-oriented knowing. We allow our deepest aspirations, yearnings, and revelations to guide us to create new forms, new social structures, and organizations in the world. We become the "future present," as is said about Jesus, claiming our inner potential as a reality, and allowing it to attract us forward to manifest in our lives.

Signs and Qualities of Youth

Following are some of the signs and qualities of our early Youth. They can act as guideposts. Add your own signs as you experience yourself entering Youth.

We Are Achieving Continuity of Consciousness as Our Essential Selves

As we enter the phase of Youth, we can remember our identity most of the time. Just as early humans once stabilized self-consciousness in the midst of an animal world, so now young Universal Humans, at the very dawn of Universal Human history, are stabilizing Essential Self awareness. Unitive consciousness is becoming a new norm. The illusion of separation rarely takes us over for long. We find that the various gradients of self-awareness—body, mind, Spirit—are flowing in a spectrum of consciousness so that we can operate fairly well at any level without separating from the other.

We can meditate and lose all personal identity within the infinite, unconditional pure awareness; we can infuse the unique "pearl" of our personal Essence with that divine intelligence, an aspect of the radiant bliss of the infinite self.

We can focus the Essential Self among the bevy of subpersonalities, egoic self-contractions, and addictive patterns that still remain from a lifetime of feeling separate, healing and making whole that which feels broken and in pain.

We can lift those weary selves up unto the peace of union with the Beloved until they forget themselves. Our local selves are our disciples. They are enjoying the pleasure of union and do not want to be separate any more.

We Are Coming into Form through Our Projects, Which Are Our Progeny, Our "Children"

In Youth, we begin to manifest our inner values in new projects, social innovations, books, works of art, organizations, political parties, enterprises, and institutions in every field that can actually assist in transforming our world. Instead of being limited by inappropriate structures, jobs, and relationships, we are actually creating aspects of the new social body. Our vocations bring forth elements of the new culture. Our genius codes, our unique creativity, even in small and almost invisible ways, are early expressions of a new society realizing its own potential for conscious evolution.

In a sense, each of our genius codes is actually a vital element of the emerging social body, just as each cell is vital to the biological body. As we make our planetary transition, each person, each member of the social body, is awakened to new functions required for survival and growth now. We urgently need to develop better social processes to find the partners to complement our own gifts. As we enter Youth, we need "vocationally oriented dating services" to help us discover our unique team.

However, in the puberty of our Youth, even if we are manifesting our creativity in important projects, we are rarely, if ever, actually able to change the larger world en masse, because most people still have not made the transition within themselves. Occasionally, an individual steps forward on the world scene as a great change agent.

Mikhail Gorbachev was such a person, but because he did not have a new culture to advocate, because he could only point to reformation of the failing communist system, or to the more apparently successful laissez-faire capitalism and individualistic democracy that was already showing its flaws and was not appropriate to the Russian culture, he could not complete his mission and was rejected. The former Soviet Union needed examples of cooperative, synergistic, win-win social models—models that have not yet been developed fully enough to serve the countries now in chaos and transition.

Nelson Mandela is perhaps the best of any transitional Universal Human in the great work of overcoming apartheid in South Africa. Yet, as Gorbachev experienced, the lingering problems that must be dealt with are so great that it is difficult for the new to emerge in the midst of life-threatening and collective egoic structures and conflicts that remain unresolved worldwide.

We Experience Vocational Arousal

In our biological phase of puberty, our hormones turn on, our bodies change, we are moved passionately to find sexual partners and reproduce the species. So in our "second puberty" as young Universal Humans, we are just as passionately aroused to find partners and join our genius to evolve ourselves and our work in the world. We move from self-reproduction to self-evolution.

As we shift from maximum procreation to co-creation, we feel the rise of suprasex. This is the awakening of our sexual drive expanding into our creative drive. In sex we yearn to join our genes to conceive a baby, while in suprasex we desire to join our genius to give birth to our greater selves and our work in the world. We may enter wild periods of "suprasexual promiscuity," where we want to fuse genius with anyone who is willing! We can't live up to our commitments. We suffer from "premature synergy," attempting to co-create before any of the partners are stable or capable in their efforts. It is difficult to remain in resonance long enough to actually create anything substantial together, very much like teenagers cannot create adult relationships and often destroy their own lives due to premature pregnancies before they are ready to be responsible.

I can remember in the early days of my Youth going to conferences and meeting kindred souls. We would become vocationally aroused and stay up all night talking about how we were going to reform education, build a new political party, create a movie . . . and then, the next morning, we could hardly remember each others' names!

Vocational arousal is the engine that fuels our natural evolution at this stage. In Youth, it becomes a dominant passion and an evolutionary driver for our own Emergence. For as we attempt to come into form with our initiatives, we hit every possible obstacle within ourselves, as well as in the world. All our weak points show up.

If the desire to express our own creativity, if the passion to join with others to co-create a sustainable viable project in the world is strong enough, we will persistently face every challenge as an opportunity to grow; we will continually transcend our self-imposed comfort limits and find that we are actualizing an immeasurable potential within ourselves and the world. It is exhilarating and joyful. We are like athletes working ourselves to the limit of our possibilities and then finding there is more to be revealed within ourselves.

A New Incentive to Free Ourselves from Ego-Driven Behavior Arises

To actually join our genius, we must be relatively free of the illusion of separation. This illusion prevents the full fusion required for the next stage of liberation of untapped potentials. Co-creation requires that we complete the Emergence Process far enough to be aware when the ego enters. For when it does, it destroys resonance and creates separation. Then, the old power struggle of dominance and submission takes hold, and judgment and fear arise.

In Youth, we are freeing ourselves from the ego's usurpation of our creativity for its own insatiable needs. Let's be humble here. The ego does not immediately disappear. It is a lifelong process of self-education and the release of self-contractions.

As we mature, our creativity begins to flow more easily, less by competition and comparisons. Our acts are increasingly self-rewarding. They express us. We feel rewarded in the doing and the being; therefore the impulse to feel driven and self-judgmental diminishes. We are transcending the dichotomy between selfish and selfless as we become self-evolving. Our greatest pleasure is our Essential Self expression and the giving of our gifts to others in the world. Our most cherished reward is the freedom to be and do our best with others.

Our work is our life's expression unfolding in tangible form through us. If we have found a way to express our life purpose, our callings in specific forms, we find that our work is the process of accessing our deeper genius and of joining our genius with others in the dance of co-creation, an extension of the lovers' dance of procreation. Our work becomes co-creation, suprasex in action. As nature put joy into sexuality to attract us to have so many babies, it is now putting joy into suprasex to motivate us to evolve ourselves and our world through connecting to create. The drives of self-preservation and self-reproduction expand into the drive for self-evolution. This drive is even now becoming, I believe, a primary force to evolve our world. In our Youth as young Universal Humans, we become world-evolvers. We are attracted and invigorated, energized and rejuvenated by our "work." In fact, our work is our cosmic connection with universal creativity.

At this stage of social life, we are rarely "hired" to perform our life purpose and must become co-creative entrepreneurs, often investing or paying our own money to do our work. We find this effort well worth it, because our life purpose expressed in chosen work is our passport to joy, companionship, fulfillment, and participation in the larger community of co-creative humans.

We Embark upon Co-creative Community

In our Youth as young Universal Humans, we move beyond occasional meetings, at conferences, churches, and events, to the formation of extended chosen families and communities of shared purpose. We begin to participate in a continuous process of co-creation through specific projects and enterprises that provide opportunity for further unfolding. Co-creative, sacred, human-scale communities begin to form. We need safe arenas to test out and experience the validity of our ideas and to stabilize our consciousness with others doing the same.

In biological evolution, mutations often occur among "isolates" that are separated from the mass of a given species. In social evolution, we need many "muddy pools," social laboratories that allow us to experiment and learn in a relatively harm-free and resonant field. Then as we mature, and as the social environment evolves sufficiently, incorporating innovations, solutions, and breakthroughs in every field, we test out our projects in the larger world. If they grow and attract resources, they are naturally selected by the process of evolution that indeed has been selecting what works best for billions of years.

We Experience Optimum Health and Regeneration

We begin to experience a sense of optimum well-being and increased energy that is a positive blessing. The alchemical process of inner union, combined with the stimulus of vocational arousal and co-creative work with others, activates the cells and infuses them with new life. Whatever age we are chronologically, as we enter Youth, we're flooded with energy that springs from the excitement of union and the passion to create. We see that our health is enhanced as the sexual drive is raised and extended into the suprasexual drive to move from maximum procreation to co-creation.

Now, in my eighth decade, I am amazed at the amount of energy that floods me every day. My strength is greater than when I was thirty, for at that time I was a seeker, I had not found my vocation or my community. I suffered from depression and feelings of failure. My local selves were signaling discontent and frustration, but the guidance had not yet emerged. I was not "plugged in" to the larger design that now floods me with vitality moment by moment.

Now this creative energy heals me of most illnesses. I find I rarely get sick. I feel as though I am almost crossing over to a new life cycle.

I am not getting older, or younger, but rather newer every day. In fact, all of us over fifty are members of the newest generation on Earth. In the past we would have been dead! Now we are living from fifty to sixty, seventy, eighty, as a new norm, feeling well, vigorous, and healthy. This is vital for the Emergence of the Universal Human. It takes a long while to grow up.

Many postmenopausal women over fifty are entering almost a new life cycle. When we say "yes" to our deeper life purpose, we actually are giving birth to the authentic feminine self. We become feminine co-creators. That is, the impulse of creativity once dedicated to reproducing the species is now available to evolve our selves and give our gift of creativity and love to the world. I have coined the word *regenopause* to describe this experience. I feel as though there is a "pause" in the life cycle. While the body is aging, the Spirit and vitality is rising. In my case I feel my very cells have been signaled that there is more for me to do. Far from sensing that my life is over, it feels as if it is emerging, that it is expressing newness again. Many women sense a greater energy and clarity than ever before. Also we often suffer from loneliness, lack of community, uncertainty as we seek our next expression in the world at a stage when we are supposed to be retiring!

The fact is we are vocationally aroused, suprasexually charged, seeking deeper partnerships. As men step outside of the structures of the patriarchy and begin to express their own essential selves, we are exploring the next level of relationship, family, partnering. If life extension is, as many biologists say, possibly offering us far longer life spans, the reproductive years will be a small percentage of our life span. Yet women's bodies are designed for the miracle of reproduction. We have hormones that turn on with pregnancy, stimulating unconditional love of the unknown child. In our postmenopausal years, when we desire to express our own creativity, we find ourselves falling in love with the unknown future, the unknown world, within ourselves and in society. It's a hormonal reserve!

Of course young women and men know that they are moving into a world filled with new crises and new opportunities. As they enter the period of Youth as Universal Humans, their creativity will be unleashed in unprecedented ways. We are all actually members of one planetary generation. No one has been through this planetary shift before. We are in it together now.

We Surrender Our Separated Intentions

In our Youth, we cease seeking status or external rewards, even the achievement of specific goals. Yes, we have intentions, but these intentions seem to be part of a larger design of which we are intrinsic participants, rather than feeling that our own separate purposes must be achieved.

We find that as we surrender and let go of our egoic notion of the way things should be, we gain a far greater freedom, released from struggling and striving to win, maturing to enjoy the process as well as the product, just as the rest of nature does. Is a tree "achieving" something as it bursts into bloom in spring? Is a baby accomplishing a goal when it opens its eyes and smiles its first smile of recognition of its mother?

In fact, the ideas of achievement and success fade because we are self-rewarded. Abraham H. Maslow called this the "Eupsychian Society," the society of self-actualizing and self-transcending people, where the greatest reward is the freedom to express what we are born to do. At this stage we are communing with other pioneering souls. We feel the union not only with those we know but also with all those souls who are now drawn by their Essence to emerge as Universal Humans, creating a vast planetary congregation from all faiths and cultures. We sense our common roots, which go back to the beginning of time and then beneath time itself into the Void, Emptiness, the Source, the Ground of Being—God.

The garden of our Youth, the Sunlit Garden of Co-creation, is really the heart of God in the temporal world, the place where people "make love" manifest in form. Through procreative love, we make babies. Through co-creative love, we make new worlds.

Journal

We have come to a shift in the Emergence Process. If you have come this far, you are at an ever-expanding threshold.

Your life purpose and genius code is turning on, you are seeking your partners, your process of co-creating. You are learning how to contribute to a new planetary culture.

As you enter Youth, in what ways do you experience this phase change? What are the fruits of this new way of being and perceiving?

As your Essential Self, write your highest purpose. State your current intention. Describe your vocational arousal. Explore the part of society toward which you would most like to contribute your genius. Ask yourself these questions:

What do I most want to create?

What do I need to create it?

What do I want to freely give?

What gifts do I have that the world most needs right now?

What gifts am I inspired to give to the Shift?

Share these questions with your friends and colleagues, reach out to people that attract you, and continue to work with the Emergence Process through all the offerings you will find on our website at *www.evolve.org*.

Welcome to the global communion of pioneering souls!

EPILOGUE

We are on a long journey together, yet this is just the beginning of our new lives and of our work in co-creating new worlds. We are a growing band of pioneering souls scattered in every culture, field, discipline, age, and background. We can have compassion for all others and ourselves. We are very young and still fragile in our ability to stabilize our identity as Essential Selves, as young Universal Humans. What is new in us is so original and imperceptible that it is often difficult to recognize what is emerging.

Since *Emergence* was first written in 1999, it is obvious that the process of change has accelerated. The global set of crises has intensified so rapidly that some observers believe we have reached a point of irreversible breakdown of our own and other species' life-support systems, through climate change, global warming, resource and water shortages, and devastation of the soil, the seas, and the very air we breathe.

It could be that our collective shifting from ego to Essence, one by one, is a decisive factor in determining which way the system goes: breakdown or breakthrough. I would not underestimate the significance of any one of us making this inner shift of identity. It is said that small islands of co-herence in a sea of social chaos can tip the system toward a more synergistic order. This is the tendency in nature. This is the Implicate Order unfolding and becoming explicate. Crises precede transformation. Nature takes jumps through greater synergy, the coming together of separate parts to make a whole greater than and different from the sum of its parts. Is it possible that as countless ones of us make the inner shift from ego to Essence and reach out to others to "join our genius," to express our creativity, *we are the tipping point in person.* Each of us!

I believe this is so. Everyone counts. Each person is a living member of the living planetary body. This whole planetary organism is itself under the stress of its emergence toward a new phase. Mother Earth gave birth to bacteria, to single cells, to animals and humans. Now she is giving birth to us, to co-creative, co-evolving humans, very young and immature, not fully knowing how to participate in a planetary shift. Yet this is the tendency of evolution. When we say *yes* to the evolutionary impulse within, when our own egoic, local selves become transparent to our Essential Selves, this impulse is rapidly coming into new form through us. As I have said, we are not doing this alone. It is not a neutral universe. It is a universe informed by exquisite universal intelligence. It is this universal intelligence that breaks through when we are sensitive to the true nature of our Essential Selves.

This is a mighty adventure, and we are the ones crossing the great divide from unconscious to conscious evolution. Our joining together in mutual support, as a global communion of pioneering souls, may indeed be a most critical factor in making the Shift in time.

Visions of the Future

To make this great journey, we need some positive visions of our own future to allure us, energize us, empower us. Where there is no vision, the people perish. Where there is vision, we flourish, we are attracted, we have something toward which to move. Visions of the future equal to our spiritual, social, and scientific/technological potential are necessary now to guide us to "cross the gap" from *here* (breakdowns) to *there* (a co-creative, sustainable, and compassionate planetary culture).

None of us can evolve fully into the stage of Universal Human Adulthood until the collective culture is transformed by us. It is our work to help create the culture that can call forth Universal Humans in the future. The challenge is huge and faces us on the personal, social, and planetary scale. It is vital for us to envision what it may be like when everything works for the evolution of life. These kinds of visions become, as I have said, magnetic attractors to guide us in the use of our rapidly expanding capacities.

What could a positive vision of our future be? There is no one answer. Here are some of the visions I see.

When and if we get through this very dangerous crisis of birth on the social scale, I envision that we will be moving toward a more "co-creative society," one in which all people will be free to be and do their best. We will have developed new kinds of social systems in every field—mind/body/spirit education, sustainable environment, clean energy, new approaches to health and healing, new forms of currency, ethical business and sustainable economics, self-organizing, nonhierarchical structures for our institutions, to name a few.

On the macrocosmic, global scale, we will have learned planetary ecological management and sustainable, regenerative economic development. In an Earth/space expanded environment, we will have access to nonpolluting, miniaturized technologies. These powers could transform the entire physical complex in which we live to one of sustainability, abundance, and unimaginable new powers, provided, of course, that we move beyond our egoic, collective misuse of these capacities.

On the individual or microcosmic scale, these new capacities, it is now being said, could evolve the very life cycle of the Universal Human beyond the familiar mammalian sequence of conception, gestation, birth, puberty, reproduction, aging, and dying. We will reach a critical phase change in the animal life cycle when we creature humans will have learned to regenerate, to live in outer space, to transform our bodies to reflect our expanded consciousness and our new environments beyond our mother planet, to increase our intelligence to an exponential degree. At this next stage, we can imagine that the higher ranges of unitive consciousness, experienced even now by a growing number, will become a new norm. At this stage of consciousness, we experience the nature of reality as divine love/intelligence and will live out our identity as that in person, in touch with many dimensions of reality.

We can envision, based on the nature of the quantum transformations that preceded us, from prelife to life, from animal life to human life, that the Adult Universal Human will emerge as something radically new yet inclusive of all that came before—an ever-evolving, co-creating, self-transforming cosmic human.

A profound question arises from an evolutionary perspective as to whether *Homo universalis* is the maturation of our own species, *Homo sapiens,* or the early stages of a new species. Here is my evolutionary intuition: We, *Homo sapiens,* are a crossover generation out of which many mutations or various speciations will appear. We will self-evolve into a diversity of species. Some will continue to live on Earth and mature the lineage of *Homo sapiens.* Others will choose to live in space, change their bodies, and build many small worlds, traveling throughout the cosmos. Some of our new capacities, like nanotechnology, biotechnology, and supercomputing, may not be appropriate in the Earth's biosphere but may be vital for a universal species in outer space. Our metaphysical preferences will become evolutionary choices. As diversity decreases on Earth, we will gain diversity in the universe. The universe is the vast "wilderness," not the Earth.

Mother Earth is giving birth to seeds of life that will flourish beyond the Earth. When Father Sun expands and destroys all the planets in our solar system, as suns always do, billions of years hence, Earth's children will be galactic beings.

The third stage on our developmental path, Adulthood, leads not to old age and death, but rather to a transition to what might be called "universal life." This is an unknown. I envision that we will become cosmic beings, spanning the galaxies in cosmic consciousness, in touch with whatever other forms of life exist in the universe, as far beyond our current stage of *Homo sapiens sapiens* as we are from *Australopithecus africanus* millions of years ago. Project us forward even a few thousand years, let's say to the fourth millennium, a blink of the cosmic eye, and we can imagine the dim outlines of *Homo universalis*, a co-creator on a universal scale.

This is one person's vision. What is yours? As we are co-creators, it is very important what we envision, because, as I have said so often, our images of the future affect reality. As we see ourselves, so we act; and as we act, so we tend to become. It is a participatory universe. There is freedom at the very core of reality. To be a conscious co-creator is not a metaphor; it is the power of metamorphosis. We are designed to know the design and to participate within it, as aspects of it, ourselves.

We are facing the unknown. Many great modern psychologists have prepared the way for our emergence as individual humans, but it hasn't been possible for anyone or any approach to fully chart this new path into the mature phases of Adulthood and beyond, because our expanded technological power of destruction and co-creation is radically new. The Universal Human we are becoming has not yet fully appeared, and so we can only point in the direction we are headed now.

To help us on our way, however, it is vital now that we develop self-images commensurate with the glorious possibilities of who we really can be. The shining beauty of the young Universal Human potentiality is hardly ever seen in the arts, films, television, and the "news." Classic science fiction writers like Gene Roddenberry, Ray Bradbury, Arthur C. Clarke, and others have at least tried to give us some visions of ourselves in the future, but rarely are they attractive enough to motivate us to realize them. The media for the most part portrays images of our failures, our weaknesses, our violent and tragic local selves. The daily "news" headlines are stories of our contending and anguished local selves. They are what Rev. Dr. Michael Beckwith calls "prayer requests."

We have not yet had our new portrait done. The Greek sculptors portrayed the beauty of young athletes and warriors, gods and goddesses, and a new image of humans was born. The medieval artists portrayed the Christ, the Virgin Mary, the saints, giving us images of divinity yet still seeing it as outside ourselves. Michelangelo sculpted the magnificent David, fully human and fully divine, yet he was unique, a hero beyond the so-called ordinary person. Modern art disintegrated this great self-image that came forth in the Renaissance. We see ourselves broken up into points of light, new forms, streams of energy, the Void. The works of Monet, Manet, Pissarro, Picasso, Jackson Pollock, and the later large blank canvases of White on White and current minimalists have revolutionized art in the modern period to portray dissolution.

We enter the post-postmodern period. I believe the most important artistic question now is, What are new images of humans commensurate with our powers to shape the future? How can art, music, literature reveal us to ourselves, alive with love and intelligence as a new norm, the next stage of human evolution? We call upon our artists to provide for us images, sounds, lights, words, poetry that evoke from us what we are becoming, that dramatize for us the Whole Story of Creation—so we can see ourselves being born as Universal Humans and a Universal Humanity. We need courage and encouragement to make the great transition.

All of us now attracted to the path of our own emergence should realize that we do not do this for ourselves alone, nor do we do it as ourselves alone. We are actually an expression of the Great Creating Process itself. The Essential Self is the personal expression of that Process incarnating in each of us, as us. We fulfill the promise given to us by great avatars, seers, and visionaries, as we embody the Emergence Process, as we mature as Universal Humans, and become conscious co-creative participants in the very process of evolution.

AFTERWORD

We are evolving closer and closer to the planetary shift. Crises deepen, while breakthroughs emerge, in our lives, in our communities, in social-change initiatives of all kinds. We are all at the threshold of what we are calling a "planetary birth experience," a phase change in human consciousness and capacities.

The Emergence Process is a vital contribution to this shift. If we enter into the larger world with our local selves in charge, we are almost sure to feel overwhelmed and are not able completely to give our gifts and realize our full potential. This is an urgently needed and foundational practice for all of us now.

Emergence in its new form is literally an expression of my own birthing process as a young Universal Human. Since I first wrote *Emergence,* my own life has accelerated. I am entering "Regenopuase" number two! At eighty-two, it feels to me that more energy is flooding through me, awakening a passionate urgency to participate more fully in the shift. In this decade there are so many more people awakening to their own *conscious* evolution that we now have a far greater opportunity to evolve ourselves and our world, in Real Time, Right Now!

I am now more than ever deeply involved in my fundamental mission: *Go tell the story of our birth as a co-creative Universal Humanity*. As one essential part of this calling, I am teaching the Emergence Process with my sister, Patricia Ellsberg. To find out more about these teachings with Patricia, as well as my many other activities, such as teleseminars, books, events, and radio programs, and to learn how you can participate with us, please go to my website, *www.evolve.org*.

GLOSSARY

Co-creative Human: a self-evolving individual who is becoming a young Universal Human, accessing the impulse of evolution, as his or her own passion to create, learning to evolve the self and the world.

Conscious Evolution: the evolution from unconscious to conscious choice; the opportunity for humans to participate consciously in the process of creation. Learning ethical conscious evolution, self and social, is the key requirement for the survival and fulfillment of our potential as a species. Our crises will lead either to transformation or to devolution and widespread extinction.

Cosmogenesis: the genesis and evolution of the cosmos from the origin of creation through the present and beyond; the new cosmology, which sets the context for our own conscious evolution.

Creature Human: the current species of *Homo sapiens sapiens*, still unaware of its own evolutionary potential; the animal/human nature of the person.

Ego: the local self suffering from the illusion that it is separate from its Essential Self. In the Emergence Process, the local self, or ego, invites the Essential Self to take dominion.

Emergence: a process of shifting our primary identity from our egoic local self to our Essential Self.

Emergence Circle: a sacred gathering of two or more to enhance our shift from ego to Essence.

Essence: a transformative agent in the process of self-realization and self-evolution, which connects us to the Godhead, the Source of all being.

Essential Self: The Beloved, the Higher Self; a unique expression of Essence, emanating such qualities as love, wisdom, wholeness, and freedom. The Essential Self is the unique and personal expression of the larger design of creation.

Genius Code: the unique gifts and talents inherent in each individual.

Godhead: the Source of all being, synonymous with many expressions such as Unified Field, Brahman, Mind of the Cosmos, Supreme Reality, Great Creating Process.

Great Creating Process: the process of creating everything that was, is, and will be; God evolving in creation. The core of the evolutionary spiral.

Homo Universalis: the next phase of *Homo* in the sequence from *Homo habilis, Homo erectus, Homo neanderthal, Homo sapiens, Homo sapiens sapiens.*

Implicate Order: the unbroken wholeness out of which everything arises not constrained by ordinary notions of space and time; the enfolded, deeper order or design of the universe, out of which the explicate order, unfolded order, is manifesting in space and time. (David Bohm)

Incarnating: the process in which the Essential Self embodies within us, responding to the local self's invitation to come in the whole way.

Inner Authority: the indwelling presence of the Essential Self, emerging in us as the wise authority.

Inner Sanctuary: the personal sacred space we create within and a physical place where we can practice the shift from ego to Essence.

Local Self: the personality self or ego that is responsible for physical survival in the material world; the generic name for the full range of subpersonalities or local selves. The local selves are sometimes constructive and often act up in troublesome or dangerous ways due to their illusion of separation from Essence. They are healed as they integrate with the incarnating Essential Self.

Noosphere: From the geosphere, the hydrosphere, and the biosphere has come the noosphere, the thinking layer of

Earth; beginning with human language and the ability to communicate, it is composed of the composite consciousness, cultures, technologies, and systems of humanity seen as a living superorganism of almost infinite power; moving toward ever-greater integration until we reach "Omega," the coming together of humans, heart to heart, center to center, for the collective rise of a critical mass of universal consciousness. (Vladimir Vernadsky, Pierre Teilhard de Chardin, Jose Arguelles)

Path of the Co-creator: the developmental path through which we shift from ego to Essence, leading to our Emergence as Universal Humans in creative cooperation with others.

Pioneering Souls: humans who are sensitive to what is emergent, who seek resonance and communion with one another in support of the planetary shift.

Planetary Birth Experience: an experience of mass coherence, connectivity, and communion toward giving birth to the next stage of our evolution as a whole planetary system.

Resonant Field: Affirming and connecting our Essential Self with the Essential Self of others, we establish a field of coherence, communion, and love that accelerates the incarnation of Essence.

Rose Chamber: a sacred and central space, a chamber of the heart within the Inner Sanctuary to cultivate the intense and blissful experience of the Union of the Human and the Divine.

Sunlit Garden of Co-creation: an extension of the Inner Sanctuary where we learn to do our work in the world with others as our Essential Self; an expanded sacred space where evolving humans learn to mature, resonate, and co-create a new world.

Suprasex: the attraction to join our genius to co-create, to give birth to our greater selves and our work in the world.

Synchronicity: the apparent acausal relationship among events; coincidences that could not be planned by human mind but that appear to flow from a larger and more comprehensive evolutionary design. (Carl Jung)

Synergy: the coming together of separate parts to form a new whole, different from, greater than, and unpredictable from the sum of its parts.

Transition: marked by the dropping of the first atomic bombs in 1945, the time on Earth when humans gained powers of co-creation or of co-destruction of our life-support systems; the period of the macroshift, when the whole system has moved far from equilibrium and could bifurcate, either toward rapid devolution and destruction or conscious evolution and transformation.

Transubstantiation: incarnating the higher frequencies of the Essential Self.

Universal Human: an evolving human who feels connected through the heart to the whole of life, awakening to the impulse to express unique creativity as an aspect of the greater design; one who experiences the cosmos as a living, interconnected, evolving, intelligent reality; our full potential self, a whole being, the fulfillment of this stage of the Emergence Process.

Universal Humanity: the civilization to be co-created by Universal Humans that manifests the harmonious integration of our spiritual, social, and scientific/technological capacities; an evolution of our species capable of co-evolving with nature and co-creating with Spirit—both on this Earth and in the universe beyond.

Vocational Arousal: the awakening of creativity, often stimulated by attraction to another's creativity as a means of fulfilling life purpose; a sign of suprasex, the expansion of sexuality into co-creativity.

BIBLIOGRAPHY

Almaas, A. H. 1986. *Essence: The Diamond Approach to Inner Realization.* York Beach, ME: Samuel Weiser, Inc.

Anderson, Carolyn, and Katharine Roske. 2001. *The Co-creator's Handbook: An Experiential Guide to Discovering Your Life's Purpose and Building a Co-creative Society* Nevada City, CA: Global Family.

Aurobindo, Sri. 1995. *The Hour of God: Selections from His Writings.* New Delhi, India: Sahitya Akademi.

———. 1999. *The Human Cycle: The Psychology of Social Development.* Twin Lakes, WI: Lotus Light Publications.

Cohen, Andrew. 2011. *Evolutionary Enlightenment: A New Path to Spiritual Discovery.* New York: SelectBooks.

Hubbard, Barbara Marx. 1983. *The Evolutionary Journey.* Santa Barbara, CA: Foundation for Conscious Evolution.

———. 1989. *The Hunger of Eve: One Woman's Odyssey Toward the Future.* 1989. Eastsound, WA: Island Pacific Northwest. (Order from Foundation for Conscious Evolution, *www.evolve.org*)

———. 1995. *The Revelation: A Message of Hope for the New Millennium.* Santa Barbara, CA: Foundation for Conscious Evolution.

————.1998. *Conscious Evolution: Awakening the Power of Our Social Potential.* Novato, CA: New World Library.

————. 2011. *52 Codes for Conscious Evolution: A Process of Metamorphosis to Realize Our Full Potential Self.* Santa Barbara, CA: Foundation for Conscious Evolution.

Jung, Carl. 1969. *Synchronicity: An Acausal Connecting Principle.* Princeton, NJ: Princeton University Press.

Lanier, Sidney. 2010. *The Sovereign Person: A Soul's Call to Conscious Evolution.* Santa Barbara, CA: Foundation for Conscious Evolution.

Laszlo, Ervin. 2006. *The Chaos Point.* Charlottesville, VA: Hampton Roads Publishing Company, Inc.

Russell, Peter. 1995. *The Global Brain Awakens: Our Next Evolutionary Leap.* Palo Alto, CA: Global Brain, Inc.

————. 1998. *Waking Up in Time: Finding Inner Peace in Times of Accelerating Change.* Novato, CA: Origin Press, Inc.

————. 2002. *From Science to God: The Mystery of Consciousness and the Meaning of Light.* Novato, CA: New World Library.

Walsch, Neale Donald. 1996. *Conversations with God: An Uncommon Dialogue,* Book 1. New York: G. P. Putnam's Sons.

————. 1997. *Conversations with God: An Uncommon Dialogue,* Book 2. Charlottesville, VA: Hampton Roads Publishing Company., Inc.

———. 1998. *Conversations with God: An Uncommon Dialogue,* Book 3. Charlottesville, VA: Hampton Roads Publishing Company., Inc.

———. 1999. *Friendship with God: An Uncommon Dialogue.* New York: G. P. Putnam's Sons.

———. 2000. *Communion with God.* New York: G. P. Putnam's Sons.

———. 2011. *The Mother of Invention: The Legacy of Barbara Marx Hubbard and the Future of YOU.* Carlsbad, CA: Hay House.

Wilber, Ken. 1996. *A Brief History of Everything.* Boston: Shambhala Publications, Inc.

———. 2000. *One Taste: Daily Reflections on Integral Spirituality.* Boston: Shambhala Publications, Inc.

Zukav, Gary. 1990. *The Seat of the Soul.* New York: Fireside.

FOUNDATION FOR CONSCIOUS EVOLUTION

The Foundation for Conscious Evolution is a nonprofit educational institution co-founded in 1990 by Barbara Marx Hubbard and Sidney Lanier.

Its mission is to educate, communicate, and activate humanity's potential for self- and social evolution. An awakened humanity in harmony with nature for the highest good of all life is its ultimate goal.

The foundation's initiatives offer a context and a container for connecting and empowering the global movements for positive change, making the efforts of this movement visible to engender greater coherence and synergy.

For a comprehensive list of the works of Barbara Marx Hubbard and the initiatives, programs and evolutionary educational offerings of the Foundation for Conscious Evolution, please visit *www.evolve.org*.

ABOUT THE AUTHOR

Barbara Marx Hubbard is the co-founder and chairperson of Foundation for Conscious Evolution. A speaker, social innovator, and author, she is focused on evolutionary education. As a modern developer of the new world view of conscious evolution, she is establishing this new field as a context for self, social, and scientific/technological evolution for the 21st century.

She lectures throughout the world and teaches seminal courses on conscious evolution for the Shift network. She also serves as a global voice for Birth 2012: Co-creating a Planetary Shift, a celebration of what is working, coherent, and creative in the world, to be inaugurated on December 22, 2012.

Her biography, *The Mother of Invention: The Legacy of Barbara Marx Hubbard and the Future of YOU,* was written by Neale Donald Walsch and published by Hay House. Her radio show, *Conscious Evolution with Barbara Marx Hubbard,* airs weekly on Hay House Radio.

She is the narrator and producer of the award-winning documentary series Humanity Ascending: A New Way through Together, which consists of *Our Story* and *Visions of a Universal Humanity.*

She is helping to form the Giordano Bruno GlobalShift University and serving with Chancellor Ervin Laszlo as a fellow in the Center for Advanced Study in Tuscany. She is the founder of the first chair in Conscious Evolution at Wisdom University.

In 1984 her name was placed in nomination for vice president of the United States, proposing a new social function: a Planetary Peace Room to be as sophisticated as our war rooms to scan for, map, connect, and communicate what is working in the world. She is currently working to bring the Peace Room into operational form.

She is a co-founder of many organizations, including the Evolutionary Leaders council, the World Future Society, and the Association for Global New Thought, and is currently a member of the Transformational Leadership Council (TLC).

She is a mother of five and a grandmother of eight.

TO OUR READERS

Hampton Roads Publishing Company
. . . for the evolving human spirit

Hampton Roads Publishing Company publishes books on a variety of subjects, including spirituality, health, and other related topics.

For a copy of our latest trade catalog, call (978) 465–0504 or visit our distributor's website at *www.redwheelweiser.com*. You can also sign up for our newsletter and special offers by going to *www.redwheelweiser.com/newsletter/*.